Teach Our Children Well

Teach Our Children Well
Essential Strategies
for the Urban Classroom

Helen Maniates and Betty Doerr
with Margaret Golden

Heinemann
Portsmouth, NH

Heinemann
A division of Reed Elsevier Inc.
361 Hanover Street
Portsmouth, NH 03801–3912
www.heinemann.com

Offices and agents throughout the world

The authors and publisher wish to thank those who have generously given permission to reprint borrowed material:

"Lessons from Home" by Lisa Delpit (interviewed by Glenda Valentine) is reprinted from *Teaching Tolerance Magazine*, Fall 1998. Copyright © 1998 by Teaching Tolerance, Southern Poverty Law Center, Montgomery, Alabama. Reprinted by permission.

Figure 7–1 reprinted from *Primary Program: A Framework for Teaching*. Published by the BC Ministry of Education, 2000. Reprinted by permission of Marilyn Chapman.

Library of Congress Cataloging-in-Publication Data
Maniates, Helen.
    Teach our children well : essential strategies for the urban classroom / Helen Maniates and Betty Doerr with Margaret Golden.
        p.   cm.
    Includes bibliographical references.
    ISBN 0-325-00387-4 (alk. paper)
    1. Education, Urban.   2. Urban schools.   3. Teaching.   I. Doerr, Betty.   II. Golden, Margaret.   III. Title.
    LC5115 .M36   2001
    371.102—dc21   2001024856

Editor: Lois Bridges
Production editor: Sonja S. Chapman
Cover design: Jenny Jensen Greenleaf
Cover photograph: Drew Story
Manufacturing: Steve Bernier

Printed in the United States of America on acid-free paper
05   04   03   02   01   RRD   1   2   3   4   5

For all our children.

Contents

Contents

Foreword

Merrill Vargo

At the beginning of the twenty-first century, as so often in the past, America is looking to its public schools. Schools today are expected to provide our democracy with informed citizens, the new knowledge economy with workers, new immigrants with access to English and American culture, and children of all races, classes, and cultures with the chance to succeed at life and work. This is nowhere so true as in the San Francisco Bay Area. Poll after poll underscores the fact that Americans understand and endorse these broad purposes for school.

Despite the importance of the role of public schools in a diverse, democratic society, and despite the consensus about this role, the current public debate about schools seems increasingly preoccupied with test scores. Standardized tests by design measure discrete skills. They can provide teachers with important diagnostic information about student needs and they can provide school systems with warning signals about skills gaps, especially among particular groups of students. What the tests cannot do is provide teachers with insights about what they can do to not only improve test scores but, more importantly, to teach students in ways that respond to the broad goals of education.

One crucial thing that teachers must do, and do well, is help students connect to school. Building a sense of community in a classroom is particularly important for students in urban settings for whom a sense of community may well be lacking. And it is particularly important in schools that, like so many in the San Francisco Bay Area, serve populations of students that bring diverse languages, cultures, and experiences to school. Connecting students to schools, to learning, and to each other is a first step in creating schools that support many more students to achieve at high levels. Some of the exercises in this book are both simple and profound. One of them asks teachers to give themselves 30 seconds to write down the first name of as many students as they can, without referring to the class list, and then complete the list, adding "something you know about each child as a person." One suspects that the forgotten or unknown students in many classrooms are our future dropouts. These are students who are neither discipline problems nor stars, and for that reason often are untapped reservoirs of both energy and intellect.

This book is intended for teachers, but it is not a training manual for building community in schools. There are many good ones out there. Instead *Teach Our Children Well* may be something more important and useful. It combines "tips and tricks" for the classroom with real stories, often in the voices of teachers and students, about how a particular strategy has impacted students. Many of the stories are memorable, and remind us all of the strength, courage, and resourcefulness of students and the joy of good teaching. Though the book is intended for teachers, it has much to teach parents about how they can better connect with their own kids. And those whose work is with adults would do well to remember the importance of building community, establishing rapport, creating a sense of belonging, and supporting others to do their personal best.

Schools that provide students with a sense of belonging often—but not always—also do so for teachers. This connection between the experience of adults in the school and the experience of children is too often forgotten. Many discussions of student achievement and school reform seem to assume that classrooms are disconnected, a sort of loose federation of independent operations. Yet the most effective schools are not this at all, but rather, as described in the vision statement of the Bay Area School Reform Collaborative, "self-consciously principled communities, committed to the growth and learning of both students and adults." The readers of *Teach Our Children Well*—teachers, administrators, parents, policymakers, or interested citizens—would do well to keep in mind the importance of building communities and creating a sense of belonging for teachers as well as students. The stories in this book remind us that it *is* possible. The third graders in Ms. Sottile's class *can* practice democracy by running their own class meeting. If we omit these activities from school, we run the risk of failing to meet our most pressing goals.

—Merrill Vargo,
Executive Director
Bay Area School Reform Collaborative

The Bay Area School Reform Collaborative (BASRC) was created in the spring of 1995 to design and manage the Hewlett-Annenberg Challenge initiative in the San Francisco Bay Area. The original five-year program has received sufficient philanthropic commitments to continue work to improve public schools for five additional years, from 2001 through 2006.

Acknowledgments

This book is a milestone in the development of Educator Consultation and Resources (ECR), a nonprofit teacher training agency in the San Francisco Bay Area formerly known as Early Childhood Resources. Founding director Nancy Kael formed ECR in 1984 to support preschool teachers' use of developmentally appropriate practice. We thank Nancy for her lifetime commitment to ensuring that all children have the chance to reach their potential. Our executive director, Jean Coppock, adroitly carries forth our mission in our current work in preschool through the elementary grades.

ECR has grown and stretched through the years and we extend our appreciation to those who developed our preschool work in prior years: John Gunnarson, Betty Rappaport, Gwen Elliot, and Harold Scoggins. Their insights into how children learn best and the personal role of the teacher in shaping a child's experience in the classroom are echoed here. As kindergarten, first-grade, and second-grade teachers became interested in student-centered practices, Kathy Rosebrock was instrumental in connecting the teaching of reading, writing, and math to our ideas about classroom environment and community, as well as helping us to develop our ideas on assessment. Her classroom has been our model and inspiration. Janet Gore, Donna Lindsay, Cheryl Nelson, and Liz Jordan have helped us bring these strategies to life for other teachers by sharing their own classroom practices through presentations and materials development.

As interest in extending ECR's work into the upper elementary grades developed, our approach changed to encompass grades three through five. Our ECR colleague Margaret Golden contributed her years of elementary teaching experience and academic training in developmental studies. Our collaboration with her formed the foundation for this book. Colombe Allen brought her wisdom and expertise to bear in the development of our thinking on classroom climate. Susan Marks provided our mirror, documenting, evaluating, and reflecting back strategies as they evolved.

We thank innovative district and school administrators, especially Kaye Burnside and Jeanne Villafuerte, for the opportunity to work with them to provide teachers the support they need to truly reach and teach their students. Special thanks must be given to the Oakland Unified School District's DAP Teacher Support Team and to the participants in the Student-Centered Learning Project with whom many of these ideas were developed. The Walter S. Johnson Foundation, the San Francisco Foundation, Maisel Family Foundation, Silver Giving Foundation, BankAmerica Foundation, and Clarence E. Heller Charitable Foundation have generously supported our work in the elementary grades.

We are forever grateful to our editor, Lois Bridges of Heinemann, whose faith in our work made this book a reality. ECR staff have all played a part in keeping our work going and in delivering this manuscript. Carola Ashford's tireless work with school administrators has been the backbone of ECR's work. Dorie Munroe, Olga Taylor, and Joy Clous provided the behind-the-scenes support that kept everything going. Deepest gratitude goes to Midge Heath for her attention to detail, good humor, and superhuman effort on this project. Shaquam Edwards, Heidi Gill, Francisco Hernandez, the entire ECR staff, and our Board have given our workplace the qualities we seek in our classrooms.

Finally, our gratitude extends to our families. Betty thanks Tim, Milagros, and Joaquin for filling her home with love; for Tim's help she is profoundly grateful. Helen thanks Larry, Zoe, and Lia for the joy and meaning they bring to her life each day.

—Helen Maniates and Betty Doerr

Introduction

As we've worked with effective teachers in urban schools, we have become convinced that a positive classroom climate, one that feels socially and emotionally safe to each child and family, is as critical to students' success in school as a strong academic program is. In fact, for many students, classroom climate is their gateway to academic engagement. In order for students to take the risks inherent in learning, they must experience a classroom atmosphere that is consistently inclusive and intellectually challenging.

Such an environment extends a sense of welcome and belonging. Each student is regarded as a unique person whose individual, family, and cultural identity is reflected in the classroom. Ideas are valued. Mistakes are regarded as learning experiences. Students are given the opportunity to build trust with the teacher and other students. Most importantly, the classroom affirms students' belief in their competence and their value as members of the learning community. We have come to the conclusion that for many students, especially those in urban settings, such an environment allows significant learning to take place where it otherwise would not.

Successful engagement in school can be thwarted when students feel that they do not belong. This can happen when teachers treat students differently on the basis of race, gender, class, or the teacher's judgment about family lifestyle. Engagement can be lost when a child's attempts to participate are ignored or when no one connects with the child as an individual. It is generally assumed that high school dropouts are unmotivated students of low ability who come from families who do not value educational achievement. Research has found that, rather than personal or family deficits, a prime factor in students' decision to drop out is a school climate that they perceive to be uncaring, racist, and unwelcoming (Wehlage 1987).

To be fully engaged in learning, students need to feel that learning will further the purposes of their lives. Without this belief, a child's natural early enthusiasm about learning begins to wane and is replaced by alienation and marginal compliance. In a community of learners, teachers support students to become independent users of the skills and concepts with which they are working, and provide authentic experiences in which to use those skills. A sense of learning for life is immediate, not deferred. As Ken and Yetta Goodman have observed,

> Traditional methods in schools may get willing students to echo verbalizations of language conventions and scientific concepts and even manipulate them in narrow and controlled contexts. But for these to become internalized and operationalized by learners—for the social to become personal—there must be room to invent, to test out, to experiment, and to reach personal-social equilibrium. (1990, 235)

Without room to invent, the Goodmans write, the classroom is "a place where you display the expected behavior by acting in acceptable ways without any real adaptation, without any real learning." David Bloome (1987) referred to this behavior as "procedural display."

Classroom community affords students the opportunity to practice being a member of an interdependent group where they have responsibilities to the other members and where their personal success ultimately depends on everyone's success. Teachers help students develop a sense of professionalism about their role as students, to know what their "personal best" means and to strive toward it. Being aware of themselves as learners allows students to actively participate in their own development, an important step on the way to becoming independently motivated, lifelong learners.

Some educators criticize learner-centered classrooms for being too soft on content, with not enough teaching going on. Lisa Delpit, author of *Other People's Children* (1995), has called the skills vs. process debate a false one because the most skillful teachers use both approaches. Responding to a similar debate, John Dewey wrote

> Nothing is more absurd than to suppose that there is no middle term between leaving a child to his own unguided fancies and likes or controlling his activities by a formal succession of dictated directions. (1902, 75)

Too much focus on climate equals summer camp; too much academic drill equals boot camp. Good teachers know it is never an either/or situation. Consciously constructing a community in the classroom allows teachers to balance the needs of the individual with the needs of the group; the need for standards with the children's developmental needs; the need for passing tests with the need to develop a love of learning and the willingness to work hard toward one's personal best. An academic program and a caring environment complement one another in a community of learners.

This book outlines an approach that draws on research methodology to develop practical strategies for creating a classroom climate for learning. The published work and lived experience of numerous teacher-researchers, cited throughout this book, have been instrumental in guiding us to best practices. The strategies we present here have evolved from those used by teachers we have worked with in the San Francisco Bay Area. Throughout the book, we note supporting research by leading cognitive theorists, professional educators, teacher-researchers, and cognitive scientists.

We construct community in the classroom for ourselves as well as for our students. We create human spaces where we can be the teachers we set out to be, teachers who can reach children. It is for ourselves, and for all teachers who urgently seek a change of climate in their classrooms and schools, that this book is written.

1

Rapport

Families entrust their most precious gift—their children—to our schools and classrooms. Parents hope they have placed their children in the hands of teachers who will know them as individuals and support them as learners. The teacher is one of the main adult role models in a child's life and the primary liaison between school and family. The teacher, through personal relationships, has the power to inspire or destroy the self-efficacy of his or her students. As observed by Haim Ginott,

> I have come to the frightening conclusion that I am the decisive element in the classroom. It's my personal approach that creates the climate. It's my daily mood that makes the weather. As a teacher, I possess tremendous power to make a child's life miserable or joyous. I can be a tool of torture or an instrument of inspiration; I can humiliate or humor, hurt or heal. (1971)

One of the first elements in the formation of a climate for learning is one that seems to be the simplest—that the teacher knows and develops a personal rapport with each child in the class.

Build Positive Rapport with Students

Third-grade teacher Cheryl Nelson reads Byrd Baylor's *The Way to Start a Day* (1986) to her class at the beginning of the year. Then, as she steps outside the classroom each morning, she greets her students, reminding them to say hello to the sun or clouds or sky as Baylor does. As she takes attendance, second-grade teacher Lyda Butler greets each child with a personal comment, such as "Good morning, Kenneth, I heard you got a new puppy this weekend!" Karen Freitas asks each student to choose a greeting from the "three H's"—handshake, hug, high-five. Liz Patterson offers the same choice. She comments,

This year everyone has chosen to hug except one student who very proudly and confidently shakes hands. This allows me to make a personal connection with every student before we begin to work. It is amazing how important this becomes for each student, and for me. I can check in with everyone and assess how the day will go. It also allows students to let me know if the day has started off rough. I have lost track of how often this greeting has changed the mood of the day, always for the better.

Kathy Rosebrock greets each of her kindergartners with a pat on the shoulder and a positive comment as they file into the classroom each day. Bee Medders starts the day with the song "It's a Beautiful Day!" Medders comments, "It gives me a chance to look into each of my students' eyes and acknowledge their presence." Retired teacher Katie O'Leary began each morning by playing Louis Armstrong's recording of "What a Wonderful World." Both Medders and O'Leary make an effort to greet each child daily.

When adults enter a room of friends or coworkers, see a relative during the holidays, or pick up a child from school, we frequently check in by asking "How's it going?" or "How was your day?" Teachers who build personal rapport with their students do the same thing—check in with each child during the school day by briefly conversing about something that's important to the child. Sometimes a teacher checks in when a child is obviously sad or angry, or seems to be affected by something that happened in the schoolyard. Checking in can clear the air by giving students an opportunity to vent and to have their feelings validated. Checking in at the beginning of the day in a whole-group circle gives students an opportunity to share their experiences and feelings as they begin the school day (Developmental Studies Center 1996).

Through an opening check-in, students reconnect with the classroom community, clear their minds, and focus on the school day. They are shifting from their experience of coming from home through the open territory of the schoolyard and into the learning community. At the end of the school day, Jen Karlen in San Francisco shakes hands with students before they leave to let them know they have her support and to make sure they leave on a positive note. When used to close the day or at the end of an activity or conflict, check-ins serve as a way to debrief and to reflect on lessons, insights, or process. Check-ins let teachers give students undivided attention and really listen to them.

Several teachers we work with incorporate other languages into their "good morning" rituals by learning to say "hello" in different ways. Donna Lindsay's kindergarten students sign in each morning next to a chart that shows "hello" in the many languages the students speak. Kindergarten teacher Keiko Chew uses students' names frequently in singing at the beginning of the year and plays name games. Chew takes students' pictures on the first day of school and uses them in games and in learning to read. Jeannette Badal uses students' photographs in her

Figure 1–1. A student copies a greeting from the multi-lingual "hello" chart.

Spanish-English bilingual kindergarten for a variety of graphing activities. Seeing their photos, hearing their names, and hearing "hello" in their own language make students feel at home in their classroom.

Alexia Tindol initiates letter-writing in her kindergarten classes by writing to each student and putting the letter in the classroom mailbox. Letter-writing and journals are a risk-free form of personal expression. When a teacher reads a student's journal, the teacher responds as another human being first and foremost. Personal notebooks go a step beyond journal entries. Notebooks have been described as a combination of diary, scrapbook, and dresser drawer. They provide a place for anecdotes, favorite quotations, poems, snatches of conversations, photos, recipes, and news clips—whatever captivates the student. In upper elementary grades, they also give students a means to celebrate their own lives at a time when outside influences and sense of self can be extremely negative.

At the beginning of first grade, students at the San Francisco School receive a black hardcover journal. Through the next eight years, students enter their footprints, handprints, self-portraits, and writing about significant events into their journals. Teachers read the journals to learn about their students' pasts and presents. At graduation eight years later, a first grader presents graduating eighth-grade students with their completed journals as they receive their diplomas.

with personal meaning in a way that would spark sharing and discussion in their classroom community, they created a large chart with clear acetate pockets and assigned a pocket to each student and each teacher. They began using the pockets by asking the children to select a special object that told a story about something that they did that summer, an idea borrowed from the infant-toddler centers at Reggio Emilia in Italy. Rappaport comments,

> With each new addition to the slowly growing assortment of objects, children showed genuine interest and enthusiasm in who it belonged to and in whose turn it would be to share and take questions. We transcribed highlights of the sharing, which we placed in the pockets with the objects.

In Sandra DeGroot's fourth-grade classroom, each student brought in a "treasure box" with an object that had special meaning. Each day one student shared his treasure box with the class.

"Kidwatching" and "kidlistening" are phrases coined by Yetta Goodman (1991) in the context of literacy learning. Whether they take the form of written anecdotal records or simple notes, the teacher's observations are critical to knowing each child. We think that kidwatching—for individual characteristics as well as for academic abilities—is the single most important thing teachers can do to build a learner-centered environment.

Gwen Elliot, preschool program director and teacher trainer, recommends a strategy called "SOUL"—S for silence, O for observing the nuances of what's taking place, U for understanding what's taking place, and L for listening to the child (Weiss 1981). As children pursue their work, adults silently observe, understand, and listen before interjecting a question or comment. Teachers give words of encouragement, building on the child's strengths and interests.

Surveys and inventories are an important way to get to know each child as a person. Etta R. Hollins (1996, 67–72) provides an excellent instrument for information gathering:

Student Data-Gathering Instrument
What I Want Most from School This Year

1. What I want most from school this year is . . .
2. It would be helpful to me in getting what I want most from school if . . .
3. The biggest problem I expect to have in getting what I want most from school is . . .
4. I might be able to overcome this problem if . . . or by . . .
5. Some places I might go for help include . . .
6. I really believe I can get what I want from school if I . . .

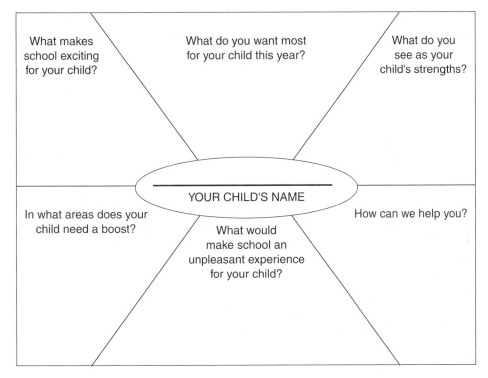

What makes school exciting for your child?

What do you want most for your child this year?

What do you see as your child's strengths?

YOUR CHILD'S NAME

In what areas does your child need a boost?

What would make school an unpleasant experience for your child?

How can we help you?

Figure 1–4. A parent survey can help to elicit parent's input on their child's school experience.

When I Think About School

1. When I think about school my first thoughts are about . . .
2. My most memorable experiences in school are . . .
3. What I like most about my present school is . . .
4. My most painful or disappointing experience in school was . . .
5. My favorite subject is . . . because . . .
6. The kind of teacher I like most is one who . . .

When I Am Not in School

1. When I am not at school what I enjoy the most is . . . because . . .
2. When I am not in school I spend most of my time with . . . because . . .
3. Of all the people I know, the one person I admire the most is . . . because . . .
4. If I could have just one wish granted, I would wish for . . . because . . .
5. If I could live any place in the world I would choose . . . because . . .

Cheryl Nelson surveys parents at the beginning of the year to learn about her students' strengths and weaknesses from the parents' point of view.

By making an effort to uncover every child's strengths, teachers can find un-recognized abilities and underdeveloped potential to build upon. Belinda Williams (1998) refers to such discoveries as a "new vision of the urban learner."

Current View	A New Vision
• deprived	• culturally different
• failing/low achieving	• unrecognized/underdeveloped abilities
• unmotivated	
• at-risk	• engaged/self-motivated
	• resilient

By focusing on a "new vision," a teacher might learn that a child who comes to school tired has a lot of responsibilities at home, such as caring for a younger sibling or older relative, or that a child who prefers to draw rather than write has a special artistic talent that can be channeled into school activities and serve as a springboard to dealing with academic tasks. A teacher can help a child connect their current interests with the future by pointing out that something the child does well is important in the adult world, such as by saying, "You really know how to make a persuasive argument; lawyers and salesmen need to be able to do that." Lisa Delpit gives a perfect example:

> I taught a six-year old who couldn't do worksheets on money. It would have been very easy for this child to be put into a special ed classroom—and I was almost ready to do that as a new teacher—because he could not do these worksheets. It wasn't until I learned about his home situation, visited his home and saw what he was capable of doing—he had to take care of his younger sister who had cerebral palsy, and he had to do the family laundry—that I realized that this was a child who was extremely competent. He could "do" money because he could get all the change needed to do the laundry; he just couldn't do a worksheet on money. He had advanced skills in critical and creative thinking but didn't have what we call "basic skills." (Valentine 1998)

If teachers get to know children personally, they can communicate unequivocal belief in each student. A recent study of kindergarten classrooms explored the relationship between students' attitudes toward school and the way their teachers interacted with them (Skinner et al. 1998). When teachers projected an image of "promise," students responded positively in terms of both academics and behavior. According to Bill Ayers (1998), "your most fundamental job as a teacher is to find the unlimited potential that you assume every child has."

The following self-reflection activity was adapted from an exercise by Donald Graves (1994) and has been useful to numerous teachers who are working on changing their classroom climate. It is designed to help teachers become aware of how important it is that they connect with every student in the classroom as a unique individual. Teachers can use this as a self-check of whether they have gotten to know each child.

Self-Reflection: Do I Know Each Child?

1. Give yourself 30 seconds (timed) to write down the first name of as many of your students as you can off the top of your head. No class lists allowed! At the end of 30 seconds, draw a line under the last name you wrote.
2. Finish the list, using as much time as you need to list all your students.
3. Look over your list. Think about why some names came up immediately and why others were harder to remember. Make a check mark next to the name of each child with whom you connected today. The connection could have been a conversation, or it could have been as simple as a kind word or glance or pat on the arm.
4. Go down your list, student by student, and write something about each child as a person. Do not write academic information, such as reading levels or test scores. Instead, jot down what a child enjoys, something about their family, or something about their special strengths or previously unrecognized abilities.
5. Review your list. Notice which children you do not know anything about as individuals and which children you have not affirmed in a positive way. Think about what you might do to remedy this. Write an "intention statement" to yourself describing how you plan to get to know this student.
6. Appreciate yourself! You have just spent several minutes thinking about each student in your classroom as an individual. You have connected with many of the students and have a plan for getting to know all the students. This personal connection will motivate you and your students to build a caring, supportive community that enhances learning in your classroom!

A hint for principals and program directors: Administrators participating in our workshops have told us that they find this a helpful exercise for learning how well they know the members of their teaching staffs as individuals. Knowing and treating each teacher as an individual helps to build a caring, supportive school community that enhances learning schoolwide.

Understand Students' Social and Cultural Contexts

Each day, students bring to school with them both in-school and out-of-school experiences that contribute to their learning. Schools have generally focused on students as separate from their communities and have ignored the interplay between individuals and their social contexts. Culture is not a set of stereotyped behaviors, but is lived as daily experience, unique to each family and child. A community of learners is created when the teacher knows students as people— knows their individual interests, values, and daily experiences.

In our own community of learners, Dr. Belinda Williams contributed significantly to our understanding of culture as "lived daily experience." According to Williams, the first step toward understanding each student involves recognizing that each teacher has a "cultural lens" through which we view our students and their families. A lens that reflects the majority culture and unconsciously represents it in the classroom may blind teachers to the richness of cultural experience that students who are not part of the majority culture bring to the classroom. Williams writes that

> Culture refers to a group's values, norms, knowledge, traditions, history, language, rituals and symbols, and interaction patterns. Culture may be described as a prism of shared meanings that enable members of a group to make sense of the world. Schools, students, and their teachers often view the world through different sides of the prism. (1998)

Culture, or lived daily experience, is the knowledge base through which a child sees the world. Rather than ignoring or making assumptions about the practices and beliefs of students' families, teachers and schools can involve families by being sincerely interested in their traditions.

At Garfield School in Oakland, California, instructional aides worked with assistant principal Kristal Chin to prepare a guide to the cultures of students' families. The pages of the guide are showcased outside the school office, inviting visitors into the many cultures of Garfield's students. Liz Jordan, who teaches a multi-age kindergarten/first-grade class, invites her students and their families to create a "heritage doll" to display in the hallway. A string connects each doll to the country it represents on a world map. Other classrooms post world maps that connect children's photos by string to their countries or continents of origin. Alexia Tindol appeals to parents by sending home a flyer that announces "cultural speaker wanted." Developing their first big unit with kindergartners around "homes," teachers Glendi Henion-Ul and James Wade take a walking field trip to each student's house. The class stands in front of the house and notices its address, color, number of windows, etc. Back in the classroom, students create a map of the neighborhood and models of their homes, make a class big book titled *This Is My House*, and do other related activities.

Teachers can cements the school/family relationship by communicating their interest in the children to parents and guardians throughout the year. Bee Medders begins before school starts, explaining that "once I get my class list, I call every single family before the year begins. I introduce myself and I welcome them to the class. I ask if there is any information they would like me to know to help me better meet the needs of their children." Fifth-grade teacher Ann Park comments, "I call every home the first or second day to let parents know how well their child has

Generally

1) Children bow down when walking past adults.
2) Children always respect their elders.
3) When handing or receiving something you do it with both hands.
4) Cambodians use soft voices.
5) Children respect teacher the same way as parents.

6) Children don't talk back to parents or teachers.
7) Children usually do not look straight into their parent's or teacher's eyes.
8) Girls are not allowed to sit cross-legged.
9) Children are not allowed to be around adults when they receive a visitor.

Figure 1–5. Instructional aides share authentic information about their cultures by creating a cultural guide for their school.

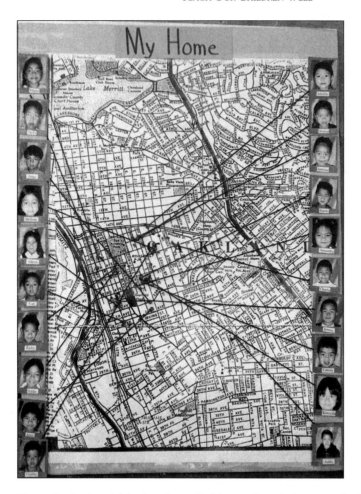

Figure 1–6. A neighborhood map linking students' photos to the location of their homes is part of the "homes" study in kindergarten.

been participating or behaving. They really appreciate this." Liz Patterson agrees and adds, "I call each student's home during the first two days of school. This is the first connection with the family. I use a 'brag about your child inventory' during the first two weeks as well as a student version in class." Kindergarten teacher Beth Coy makes it a point to talk briefly to at least one parent about their child each day when students are being picked up at school. Coy comments that "parent conferences aren't usually scheduled until after nine weeks of school, but I start scheduling mine after four weeks, so I can have time to talk with the parent and get to know the parent in a positive way." Kathy Rosebrock has found beginning-of-the-year conferences focused on parental input to be invaluable for getting to know parents' expectations and concerns.

"This is my house," said Stephanie.

Figure 1–7. Kindergartners create a big book of paintings of their homes with the repeated refrain, "This is my house."

Liz Jordan sends this note home to parents at the beginning of the school year:

A Note from Ms. Jordan

In her book *A Sense of Wonder*, Rachel Carson wrote:

> I sincerely believe that for the child, and for the parent seeking to guide him, it is not half so important to know as to feel. If facts are the seeds that later produce knowledge and wisdom, then the emotions and the impressions of the senses are the fertile soil in which the seeds must grow. The years of early childhood are the time to prepare the soil. Once the emotions have been aroused—a sense of the beautiful, the excitement of the new and the unknown, a feeling of sympathy, pity, admiration, or love—then we wish for knowledge about the object of our

Small Group Time News
My Kindergarten Journal

The children are excited to have begun their journals. Each child has his or her very own spiral-bound notebook to use throughout the year; in June the journal will be brought home to keep. Your kindergarten child is already an enthusiastic writer! Just as in learning to walk and talk your child is growing in stages of learning to write.

Infants and toddlers want to pick up pencils and crayons to make marks and lines on paper. These are their "baby steps" in their development of using written language. Preschoolers and kindergartners scribble, draw, make pretend letters and words, and might created temporary or unconventional spellings to communicate their ideas and feelings.

We value greatly the children's own writing. We recognize the importance of each child writing at his or her own stage of scribbling, drawing, or making letters and words. We support the children by complimenting them for their successes and by providing an environment that helps each one move forward on to the next appropriate stage.

Here are some samples of Kindergarten writing:

You can help your child at home by providing TIME TO WRITE. Make available a variety of paper, pencils, crayons, markers, scissors, and glue. Model writing by allowing your children to watch you make lists, pay bills, and write letters and messages.

Figure 1–8. Curriculum is shared with parents through newsletters such as "Small Group Time News."

emotional response. Once found, it has lasting meaning. It is more important to pave the way for the child to want to know than to put him on a diet of facts he is not ready to assimilate. (1956)

And with that, I feel fortunate to begin with your children on the journey of excitement, joy, and love of learning throughout the curriculum and in the world beyond.

Teachers can demystify the world of school and bring parents in as partners in several easy ways:

- Call parents at the beginning of the year.
- When parents drop off or pick up their children, take the opportunity to talk with them, if only briefly.
- Use the first conference to ask parents how they would like to help their children, and how they would like you and the school to help their children.
- Ask parents to fill out surveys at the beginning and end of the school year.
- Give parents a handbook that describes your curriculum and classroom traditions and answers frequently asked questions.
- Update parents on class activities through weekly or monthly newsletters.
- Ask parents to sign homework and comment on it.
- When a struggling student has had a particularly great day, have him call home from the office to tell about it.
- Use phone calls or notes home to tell parents about observations, funny anecdotes, and concerns that students have shared.
- Write a compliment on a sticky note and put it on a student's homework packet.
- Ask parents to participate in lots of little and big ways: read to their children; send in cultural artifacts such as clothing, recipes, or dolls; sit in on the class; read or tell the class a story or share a life experience.

Teachers acknowledge the richness of students' experiences outside of school by integrating home life and school life. When the teacher acknowledges and values home experiences, children feel a sense of coherence between their two worlds. The skills they bring from their home lives can be used to help them succeed in school. Williams and Woods have found that urban students learn best when the school's environment, curriculum, instruction, and assessment overlap with the culture/community's traditions, daily experiences, language, and values (1997).

Glendi Henion-Ul, a teacher at Garfield School in Oakland, reflects on her experience in the community:

There's something I am discovering about having been at Garfield for as long as I have now which I think is related to community in a broader sense. When I walk into any of the housing projects, people know who I am even if they don't know me directly. Although I do not live in the immediate community, I am more accepted because I have stuck around for a while. There's something rewarding about that. I think this year I already knew more than half of the students who came into my classroom from siblings or relatives, or friends of students I have taught. I have been in and out of their homes and lives for a number of years now, have gone to weddings, birthday parties, and funerals with them, so it feels like some of that gap from not residing in the community has been bridged.

Helping students connect what they know from out-of-school experiences with new concepts being introduced in school is one of the most powerful inducements to learning. When third-grade teacher Charlotte Harrell became aware that some of her students had a lot of experience performing oral recitations through their church activities, she began to have students memorize and perform poetry and stories in the classroom. Shaquam Edwards used familiar songs and chants like "Miss Mary Mack-Mack-Mack, all dressed in black-black-black" to teach phonemic awareness.

Writers—including student writers—write best about what they know well. Writing assignments that draw on the family's history and culture bring student, parent, and teacher together as parties who are interested in the child's learning experience. Gathering stories from home gives students a powerful life experience, and the stories themselves can be studied across the genres. And when teacher and students share their life stories and experiences, it helps build the classroom community.

Over the past few years in her kindergarten/first-grade classroom, Sally Feldman has compiled a class book titled *My Name Is Special*. With each new class, Feldman sends home a note asking parents to write a brief statement about how they named their child. She types up the statements and designs a page for each child, with the child's name in large print surrounded by a border chosen just for them. After the students color in their names, these pages are added to a comb-bound book that is kept in the classroom library. Students enjoy reading and rereading about their own names and the names of their friends. As new readers start learning names, they practice reading the name book. Upper elementary students come back to visit their old kindergarten and find their names as well. Through this activity, students learn about one another. The name book gives Feldman a special connection to each child and family. As she says, "it has made me so aware of how loved the children are."

Ann Park uses the following questions when her fifth graders research their names:

- What is your full name?
- Were you named after someone? If so, whom?

Jazmelina got her name from the flower, Jasmine, and her grandmother's name, Melina. We took the two and combined them together and got Jazmelina. The Jasmine flower is my favorite and that is why I chose the name.

Figure 1–9. Jazmelina's mother explains how she created her special name.

- Does your name have a special meaning?
- Do you have a nickname? What is it and how did you get it?
- What is your ethnic background/culture?
- Tell me something special about your culture.
- What are you most proud of about your culture?
- What are you most proud of about yourself?

Assignments that help students learn their own family's oral history and favorite stories connect them to their cultural heritage. Personal stories that are different from our own bridge the divides that separate us. Students can create timelines with their parents or guardians that showcase their own accomplishments ("walked at twelve months") or the life of the family. Teachers can help make students' sense of historical time more concrete by relating family timelines to events in history.

In Wendy Smithers' third-grade classroom, the first few weeks are spent on family history, with projects that involve students and parents. Projects include interviewing parents and writing about family traditions, goals, favorite recipes, lineage and family trees, and stories told by grandparents. Smithers notes, "the study of family history makes a direct tie-in to our History of South San Francisco unit. It gives students time to reflect on their own past as we go into the past of our town."

When students write about their heroes, their role models, or "wise ones," they can ask parents or other family members a focus question such as "Who

Ndikho's name came from a friend of Ndikho's grandfather who actually was a South African Freedom Fighter. Ndikho's name is an African name that means 'Son of a Dreamer.' The name was first given to Ndikho's father, whose father named him. I knew that if I ever had a son, he would be given this name that holds a very special place and meaning in my heart. When I gave birth to my very first child, I knew for a fact that he was a 'Son of a Dreamer,' for that is the meaning of my little loved one's name.

Figure 1–10. The history of Ndikho's name is told by his mother for the class book.

are your heroes, and why?" Interviews with parents or grandparents and student autobiographies become treasured gifts and can make their way into news articles, cookbooks, memoirs, poetry books, class books, and social studies projects.

Relationships are not one-sided; they do not come about as a result of one person or group's entrusting their dreams and fears to a silent "other." Developing a relationship with each student and family means that we as teachers must share ourselves with our students. We watched Sandra DeGroot explain to her class that their student teacher and a new student from Russia were leaving their classroom. She spoke to her students about what it meant to say goodbye, describing how she had just said goodbye to her eighteen-year-old son as he left for college. She then invited her students to silently reflect in their journals about a time when they had to say goodbye. By sharing ourselves, telling our own stories, and speaking about our own daily experiences, teachers can transform our classrooms from impersonal settings to communities of learners.

2

Traditions

When visiting teachers see students at work in a community of learners, they often ask themselves, "How did she *do* that?" It can appear that an exceptional teacher has encountered an exceptional group of students, and the results are a reflection of that unique combination. Yet all classrooms have the potential to be powerful communities of learners. Traditions, transitions, and work routines are the mortar that gives strength to student-centered classrooms and enables students to function successfully throughout the day.

Ritualize Transitions

Vera Nobles' third-grade students in Point Richmond, California, sing a traditional Swahili school song to open the day, making a cultural connection with students' heritage. Robert Marosi, a Spanish-English bilingual fourth-grade teacher in San Francisco, opens the day sitting at a table near the door, coffee cup in hand, paging through the morning paper, a group of students circled around him. Students enter and filter by the table, checking in informally with one another or Robert, or checking out the day's news. After all students have entered, Robert launches the day. He feels it is important to take a few minutes to create a homelike social atmosphere as his students transition into the day. Liz Jordan starts the day in her kindergarten/first-grade classroom with parents and children reading together on the rug. A fifth-grade teacher in Hayward, California, opens the day sitting in an armchair. She quietly lights a candle and begins by reading a story or poem to her students. She ends the circle by briefly describing the day, then blows out the candle, signaling the beginning of an active day.

Students Transition from Home to School

Beginning with a welcoming routine such as a special song, greeting, sequence of whole-group activities, or a morning meeting provides a secure, familiar way for students to settle into the day. Gathering as a community rather than going silently to their desks and beginning on individual work establishes a sense of welcome and belonging on a daily basis.

Beth Coy's classroom community starts each day with morning meeting (Charney 1992). Coy and her students stand in a circle. Turning to her right, she shakes hands with the student next to her and says, "Eric, I'm glad you're here today." That child then turns to his right and greets the next child, who greets the next child, and so on until the welcome returns to Coy. They sit down for morning meeting, and Coy raises a question for the day. "In the beginning of the year it is a getting-to-know-you question such as 'What do you like to do at home?' Later in the year the questions are about the theme we are working on."

A morning meeting is a daily ritual that sets the tone for the day. It is a centering time, full of anticipation for a day of positive shared experience. Students are greeted and individually recognized as being present. Liz Jordan's morning meeting is typical:

1. Jordan welcomes each child individually.
2. The class sings a "good morning" song.
3. Teacher and students discuss the day to come.
4. Students do a whole-group math activity.
5. Students pick the "teacher of the day" using Popsicle sticks with names written on them. (The "teacher of the day" takes attendance, is "Inspector Gadget" for clean-up time, and gets special "homework.")

When kindergarten students enter Glendi Henion-Ul's classroom, she greets them, then they file their homework, choose a new take-home book, and mark their own attendance by placing a colored clothespin on a large name chart that also serves as a tool for math and graphing activities each week. Henion-Ul might post an interview question such as "Do you have laces on your shoes?" above the chart. Students with laces sign in with blue pins and those without laces sign in with peach pins. The class then tallies the pins and records the result on a large graph. The name chart has a picture of each student, and it is also used for many community-building and language arts activities. After marking attendance, the students choose a book from book tubs around the room, while the "person of the day" records attendance. Henion-Ul holds a meeting each morning, focusing on three class norms for the meetings: Attentive Listening, No Put-downs, and the Right to Pass (Gibbs 1995). She sometimes suggests a topic, especially in the beginning of the year (favorite food, number of siblings, what makes you happy or sad). Often the meeting is open, or the person of the day chooses the topic.

The format of the morning meeting can be as individual as the teacher. Some teachers incorporate singing or reciting. Some have students pass a formal "good morning" around the circle, share special events of the day, or introduce the "word of the day." Kathy Rosebrock draws on children's home experiences by using interactive writing techniques to take down their "daily news."

Keiko Chew opens her kindergarten morning meeting with songs, such as "Say Hello." "I like the part in the music that encourages us to shake hands. Then I start the meeting with a phrase, 'I feel…' Students who don't want to share can say, 'Pass.' I use cards with students' names, and they take turns as their name appears."

Bee Medders uses a name chart to take roll in her kindergarten class. As students are called on, they greet the class in one of many languages and the class greets them back. When a student is absent, the class sings, "Where is_____? Where is_____? She's not here. Where can she be? Where can she be? She's not here." Students know that even if they are absent they are acknowledged. When the student returns, the class tells her how glad they are that she is back and how much they missed her.

Guidelines for Morning Meetings
- Keep them short.
- Have a shared understanding of how students will be seated.
- Include grade-appropriate content—news, weather, items to share, announcements, unfinished business, upcoming events or activities, and the day's schedule.
- Have a routine way to take turns—pass an object (talking stick, class mascot) or roll a ball, and let each person speak before there is a repeat.
- Establish rules that demonstrate respect for one another, such as listening to the speaker, making eye contact, and not putting other students down.
- Make the meeting meaningful—if some students need more time to share, ask others to give them their time.
- Include an element of ceremony—a special song ("Imagine," "What a Wonderful World"), a candle, music—that brings the group together.
- Keep it fresh—include role-playing, poetry, songs, news articles, and art.
- Limit or eliminate sharing about movies, television shows, and toys.
- Avoid a competitiveness by inviting students to share objects related to a new discovery, experience, or current classroom theme.

Listening, responding, and taking turns influence the quality of the meeting. How students take turns varies from class to class. Students might roll a ball across the floor, toss a beanbag, or pass a small rain stick, a rock, or a stuffed animal. Expecting students to actively listen to each other with no interrupting or hand waving and giving them the "right to pass" teaches them to respect one another and contributes to a lifelong habit of listening before speaking.

Seating arrangements seem like a small detail but can affect the quality of a meeting. We have seen a meeting break down because one student was in another student's "space" or because a student accidentally brushed another's arm. We have also witnessed classrooms where the teacher sat down and waited in silence. Within a minute the other students had followed suit. The teacher glanced around the circle and said, "Steve, please change places; Margo, change places." She knew her students, knew who would be tempted to distract others. The whole process happened seamlessly, within two minutes. Some teachers ask each student to bring a cushion to sit on. Others have students sit cross-legged, with hands in lap; still others have some students sit on a table at the edge of the circle when more space is needed. In upper-grade classes and large classes where there is no rug area or large open space, students have a routine for quickly moving tables or desks aside to make room for the meeting.*

Students' Transition from School to Home

Exit slips, class chores, homework review, and meetings about how the day went prepare students to return home or transition to after-school activities. Students can report "daily news"—major occurrences or lessons learned during the day. Second-grade teacher Nameeta Tolia-Henbest ends each day by reading aloud, sending students off on a calming note.

Many classrooms mark the end of the week with a Friday routine that acknowledges the hard work the students have done. This might be a longer "choice time" for exploring classroom materials or a "finishing-up time" for completing work and getting a feeling of closure about the week's activities. Sometimes more pleasurable daily routines, like chapter book read-aloud or students' reading their writing to their peers get lengthened. "Daily news" can become the content of the "weekly news," along with announcements or student writing or art. The weeks' events can also be recorded in a class history book, with students alternating turns as class historian. This can be a time for journal writing, with students reflecting on the past week and thinking through the days ahead. Formal closure is especially important to students who face weekends that may be filled with anxiety and confusion.

---

* *Responsive Classroom: A Newsletter for Teachers* focuses on the social curriculum in the classroom and provides ideas for morning meetings and much more. Published quarterly and free to teachers, it is available through the Northeast Foundation for Children at www.responsiveclassroom.org.

Celebrate Transitions Throughout the Year

The school-year transition represents so much in a child's life—growing a year older, passing to the next grade, becoming a "big kid" a little at a time. These are major life events for parents as well, and their hopes and anxieties for their children often get played out at these times. Classroom traditions can ease anxiety around the school-year transition and provide a sense of anticipation and well-being.

Beginning a New School Year Is a Major Transition

At West Portal School in San Francisco, parents of incoming kindergartners bring their children to visit. Teachers welcome parents' requests and recommendations, for example, that a new student be placed with the same teacher her sibling had. New families are invited to a welcoming brunch hosted by veteran families on the first Saturday of the school year. Parents are invited to a welcoming coffee on the first day of school.

Teachers who receive their class lists before the year begins often send postcards to incoming students to introduce themselves and let the students know how much they look forward to the school year. Receiving a piece of personal mail is momentous for a child, and hearing from the teacher is very special. The postcards give children a little forewarning that vacation is coming to an end and school will soon be a reality. The caring demonstrated by the postcard is very reassuring to parents, too—it lets them know that the teacher is interested in their child.

At the beginning of the year, students get introduced to all the routines and expectations of the new class and the teacher's attention is focused on both curricular and social goals. As with other goals, students need concrete demonstrations and learning situations to develop social skills.

Throughout the school year, there are times—preparing for a substitute; before and after holiday breaks—when social skills again become the focus. At such times, teachers can use class meetings to have students review class norms and expectations, role-play possible scenarios, and brainstorm solutions and other issues. The same can be done when unexpected changes in or out of school influence the learning environment. Natural disasters, death, crime, even changes in the weather may call for reflection and a renewed focus on social skills.

The End of the Year Evokes Relief and Loss

The familiar, comfortable routine of the classroom and its community gets dismantled as the school year draws to a close. As teachers approach the end of the school year and are involved in finishing up projects and units of study, they can help

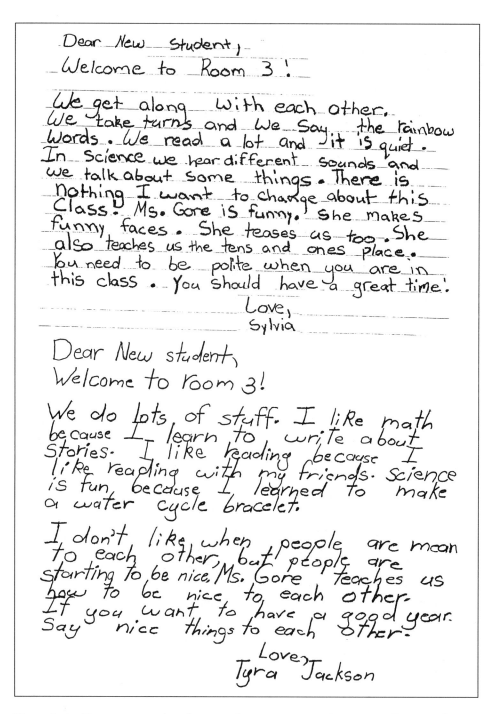

Dear New Student,
Welcome to Room 3!

We get along with each other.
We take turns and we say the rainbow
words. We read a lot and it is quiet.
In science we hear different sounds and
we talk about some things. There is
nothing I want to change about this
class! Ms. Gore is funny. She makes
funny faces. She teases us too. She
also teaches us the tens and ones place.
You need to be polite when you are in
this class. You should have a great time!
                                    Love,
                                    Sylvia

Dear New student,
Welcome to room 3!

We do lots of stuff. I like math
because I learn to write about
stories. I like reading because I
like reading with my friends. Science
is fun, because I learned to make
a water cycle bracelet.

I don't like when people are mean
to each other, but people are
starting to be nice. Ms. Gore teaches us
how to be nice to each other.
If you want to have a good year.
Say nice things to each other!
                        Love,
                        Tyra Jackson

Figure 2–1. Outgoing second graders write letters to next year's incoming class to welcome them to the classroom.

students acknowledge the transition by reflecting back on the year. Second-grade teacher Janet Gore describes her classroom:

> In my classroom, I am always working on making transition times run more smoothly. I want my students to finish activities with a sense of closure, and I want them to approach new experiences with positive anticipation. I try to help my children welcome change and feel that they have a sense of control over their day. Similar considerations need to be made around other transitions that occur in the school year.
>
> One potentially dramatic time is promotion to the next grade. Although we as teachers often welcome the end of the year and the fresh start in the fall, children sometimes have very real concerns: Who will my teacher be? Will I like her? What will the class be like? Will I fit in?
>
> One way to help children adjust is to have the previous class write letters to the new one. In the spring I have each of my students write about what they think a new person to the class should know. They include what they like (and don't like) about the class, the daily routine, what the teacher is like, and some words of advice. I mail the letters early in the fall, and the new class has the excitement of receiving real mail and learning some usually very positive, reassuring information about their new "home."

Highlighting the phases of the school year and the phases of learning can make students conscious of the learning process while adding to their feeling of having a shared experience.

Create Classroom Traditions

Every community celebrates through traditions, recognizing effort, achievement, seasons, the passage of time. Classroom communities mark significant events in the lives of class members and the class itself through traditions that draw students together. These events help students to see themselves growing and changing. Ralph Peterson describes this eloquently in *Life in a Crowded Place*:

> Just as painters work with the elements of point, line, tone, and plane, teachers and students use ceremony, ritual, rite, celebration, play, and critique when they are making a learning community. These elements are as old as humankind. When students do routines and chores, celebrate, converse with one another, engage in rituals and ceremonies, and give and receive criticism, they are doing what is an everyday part of their lives. The living and learning that occurs in the classroom is shaped by the same cultural forms humankind has developed over the ages. (1992, 13)

Janet Gore describes the importance of traditions to her second-grade classroom community:

> Traditions define a classroom and give kids a sense of pride and belonging. They ritualize the everyday routine and celebrate events throughout the year. Traditions are not necessarily momentous observances; they are sometimes seemingly insignificant practices that give a classroom its unique identity and validate kids' membership in a special group.
>
> Both teachers and kids are responsible for establishing traditions. Some come from deliberate planning and others just seem to happen. Many live from year to year and become trademarks of a particular classroom. In my second-grade classroom this year we have a silly tradition we call "safety control." One day we were working with markers and I reminded the students to put papers down to protect the desks. One of my students sang out "safety control!" We all laughed, and we laugh each time we get out "safety control" papers. This tradition is like our own personal secret and we all feel close as we share it.

Song Detoc's classroom has a special welcoming ritual. When she learns that the class is going to have a new student, Detoc brings it up for discussion in morning meeting. Students talk about how it might feel to be new: "scary," "brave," "lonely." The upcoming event gets reported in the "daily news." During writing time, students write letters welcoming the new students to the class. They write about how difficult it must be to move, how brave the student must be for doing it, how they would like to be his friend. The letters are bound and made into a class book that is presented to the new student as he arrives, welcoming him into their community of learners.

Sally Kaneko's first-/second-grade classroom has a tradition, called "clump," for showing appreciation to students who read at story time. After the reading, the class counts to three in one of the students' home languages, then yells "CLUMP": "ichi, ni, san, CLUMP."

Using a sandtray—a large wooden tray filled with sand and a variety of miniature figures—is a tradition in third-grade teacher Laura Burges' classroom.

> Many children through the years have donated objects to the sandtray collection—which includes houses, cars, human figures, trees, animals, etc. One of the third graders said to me, "I will feel good when I'm in college, knowing third graders are still using my things in the sandtray."

Burges gives each student the opportunity to work in the sandtray a few times a year, working her way through the class list and giving students the right to pass.

> A child will work independently and in private to create a scene in the sandtray during morning meeting or silent sustained reading so lessons aren't missed. When

the sandtray is completed, I will find a quiet moment to meet with the student, since children often want to describe what has happened, telling the story they have created in the sand.

Burges gives each child a quiet, private time to create a story, free from judgment, praise, or pressure to create a product. The students cherish their sandtray work as a special "quiet time," and sometimes ask permission to come in at recess or another time to have an extra moment with the sandtray.

Nancy Sarraga, a first-grade teacher, describes how important using a sandtray is to her students:

> As the children mature at our school, more and more is expected of them academically. The sandtray is an opportunity for a child to be in the midst of class while working independently, choosing objects that suit the moment, playing with the sand, building mountains and rivers, forests and towns. When a child meets with me, he or she is confident of my undivided attention as I "capture" and take care of his or her story. It is a unique and invaluable conduit of trust and respect that I can share with each child.

Wendy Smithers' classes celebrate the Mexican Day of the Dead in many ways, changing with each class. Her third-grade students buddy with an upper-grade class, build "altars" for loved ones who've died, and write and read about family members who have passed on.

During December, many classrooms develop traditions that celebrate holidays. In her book *White Teacher* (2000), kindergarten teacher Vivian Paley writes about how she, a Jewish student, felt when her teachers assumed that everyone celebrated Christmas. Paley describes her own struggle as a teacher to speak openly about cultural differences in the classroom. To address culture authentically and realistically, she needed to ask her students' parents what they valued and wanted to communicate about their culture. Without such information from parents, teachers often treat cultures in a way that is superficial, stereotypical, and even inaccurate.

In her monthly newsletter to parents, Liz Jordan acknowledges their role in creating an authentic experience of traditions.

Thank You, Thank You

During the month of December, several parents assisted in our classroom and taught the children about traditions that they celebrate or have celebrated. Mrs. Kim taught us about Korean New Year celebrations. Mr. Pavicac taught us about the holidays in Croatia, Mrs. Charleson shared Hanukkah traditions, and Mrs. Whipple taught us about the principles of Kwanzaa. Mrs. Sandoval shared Mexican traditions that we celebrated with a piñata. Mr. and Mrs. Balazs brought a Filipino star into our classroom. It was a wonderful month, culminating with a very delicious feast that you all made happen. Thank you so much for all that you do!

Traditions and transitions are as different as each classroom's teacher, students, grade level, and sense of community. What communities of learners have in common is a sense of tradition that binds teacher and students together.

Classroom Traditions

- morning meeting
- singing
- poetry reading
- class newspapers
- class yearbook
- class poetry book
- reading aloud
- student of the week
- author's chair
- end-of-the-day reflection
- newcomer traditions
- end-of-the-year reflection
- special meals
- promotion ceremonies
- birthdays
- family nights
- author nights
- class museums
- curriculum celebrations
- special-day celebrations planned for the whole school

Promote Schoolwide Traditions

Schoolwide traditions can be as complicated as holding an all-school author's night or as simple as opening the school year by having each student do a painting of the same object—"hats," "cats," and so on. Art teachers Karen Goodkin and Karen Klimak cover the walls with these paintings, each signed by the student. Teachers, students, and parents stop to gaze at them, noticing differences in style and technique and the uniqueness of each and identifying the paintings done by their siblings, children, and friends.

Music teacher Doug Goodkin discusses all-school traditions:

The celebration calendar of the San Francisco School is an integral part of who we are. It recognizes that joy is essential to the learning process and helps move mere information to transformation through celebration. It puts community in the center of the learning environment as both an active component and beneficiary of that environment. Festive group sharing helps complete a cycle of learning while simultaneously stimulating the next step up the spiral. Finally, our celebration calendar states that it is vital to both individual and community health to publicly acknowledge important moments—beginnings, welcoming, transitions, endings, farewells and issues-suffering, exploitation, struggle, triumph. Many stories from alumni confirm that this aspect of school life has long-lasting effects. Our students often move on to situations in which they create ceremonies in their later schools, jobs, and lives, inspired by the model that we offer.

On the first day of school at the San Francisco School, each grade enters from the playground into the assembly room through an archway of flags held by parents. Teachers play music to welcome the students. When all the students have assembled, they sing their welcome song, together and as a round. The school's principal, Terry Edeli, welcomes the students with short remarks, then invites the oldest and youngest student to come forward and open the year, with the youngest ringing a small gong and the oldest ringing a large gong. One student from each grade level comes forward and receives an empty glass. The oldest student fills the glasses in order, from oldest student to youngest, to represent the passing of knowledge and experience. To represent openness and the spirit of inquiry, the youngest student then takes the pitcher and moves up the line collecting the water. The students then sing "Simple Gifts."

Edeli speaks about the importance of caring for the classroom, the school, the community, and the Earth, and asks the eight students to hold high a large globe. The whole student body sings "Earth Day Rap," written by Doug Goodkin. Students are dismissed to their classes to the applause of the school community, exiting from youngest to oldest. From year to year, parents watch their children walk through the same door and see how much larger they have grown.

Earth Day Rap

The sky is high and the ocean is deep
But we can't treat the planet like a garbage heap.
Don't wreck it, protect it, keep part of it wild.
And think about the future of your great grandchild.
Recycle, bicycle, don't drive by yourself.
Don't you buy those plastic products on the supermarket shelf.

Boycott, petition, let the big business know
That if we mess it up here, there's nowhere else we can go.
Don't shrug your shoulders and say, "What can *I* do?"
Only one person can do it and that person is YOU!

When she was principal of Washington School, Kaye Burnside started a tradition of opening the day with a brief all-school assembly that has continued. Birthdays are recognized and student achievement awards in both the social and academic arenas are given. Letters to the school are read and songs are sung. The word of the week is announced. Everyone recites the Washington Pledge, reaffirming each child's potential and the power of the school community. At School of the Madeleine, principal Mitch Calegari holds an all-school ceremony each morning, talking to students about the values of kindness and cooperation on which the school is built. Students turn to each other in pairs and say, "Let's be good to one another today." The whole school then exclaims, "Pass it on!" Alvarado School has a "birthday bash" during which all children whose birthday is that month receive a book and a birthday card. Students at Lawton School receive a ribbon that says "It's my birthday" at morning assembly and wear it all day long. All-school singing is a powerful way to build a sense of community across grade levels. The school can sing at morning openings, once a week at assembly, or every day for fifteen minutes after lunch. As the school develops its own repertoire of "oldies but goodies," students feel a connection across the grades.

Seasonal events offer opportunities to create schoolwide traditions. West Portal School holds a "family pumpkin patch" with decorated classrooms and time scheduled for families to come to the classrooms to buy pumpkins. Students, teachers, and principal Jeanne Villafuerte dress up for a Halloween parade. Thanksgiving is the time for the traditional feast in kindergarten and first grade. Families—including siblings—are invited. Families are invited to contribute to an annual food drive. The school holds a holiday sing-along in December with a choral group from Washington High School. Everyone gathers at West Portal for a light dinner, and the choral group brings cookies to share. Parents, students, and teachers sing together at the school, then walk down West Portal Avenue singing together. Participating in San Francisco's Chinese New Year parade has been a school tradition for fourteen years. Over a hundred students participate each year, making a commitment to Friday and Sunday rehearsals that begin in November. The West Portal School contingent includes drummers, stilt walkers, lion dancers, and ribbon dancers. Principal Villafuerte plays a drum. Over the years, the school has won first and second place. After the parade, families return to school for a Chinese dinner. Shortly after Chinese New Year, the school holds a spring festival fundraiser where the groups from the parade perform and school groups sell items.

On the last day of school, students at the San Francisco School eat ice-cream sandwich mud pies in their classrooms and sing the "Mud Pie Song." The whole school then gathers in the assembly room and sings "Skinnarmarink" and "Que Sera." The all-school ceremony, called "gonging up," advances students to the next grade level at the sound of a gong, as each teacher moves to next year's group of students. Students feel a sense of pride, accomplishment, and anticipation as they change grades. Fifth-grader Ben Pepin describes the last day of school:

> One of the best days of school is the last day because we get to eat mud pies and we have no homework. It is also kind of fun. Some weird people don't like the last day because there is no school the following day. I think those people are crazy. Another good thing about the last day of school is that we get to move up a grade. This year that's very exciting because we are going to be sixth graders and that makes us cool middle schoolers!

Fifth graders at West Portal finish elementary school with a rite of passage. Parents, students, and teachers watch a slide show of the class through the years. Families whose youngest child is leaving the school are honored with bouquets of flowers. Students and their families leave the school knowing they have been valued members of the school community.

Schoolwide Traditions
- opening-day ceremony
- back-to-school potluck
- life books
- cross-age tutoring
- student art exhibits
- student murals
- published writing displayed
- fifth-grade or eighth-grade gift to the school
- all-school meetings
- all-school singing
- all-school walkathon
- fairs for special occasions
- all-school government (with community projects to work on)
- storytelling night
- heritage week
- family heritage museum
- family projects fair
- academic fairs

- grandparents' day
- school community garden
- schoolwide recycling project
- giving thanks (selecting a staff person, interviewing them, thanking them)
- tree planting day
- family work weekend
- all-school performances

3

Pride of Place

A classroom that reflects community is imbued with an atmosphere of welcome and belonging. The organization of the physical environment and the choice of materials reflects the educational philosophy of the teacher and the school program. The arrangement of the desks, the relative prominence of the teacher's desk, the accessibility of materials, and the type of materials available relay a silent message. The way the space is used suggests the activities students will engage in and whether students will mostly work in a whole group focused on the front of the room or in small groups interacting with one another. It reflects whether students will sit for most of the day or move around the room using areas set up for different purposes.

An organized classroom functions as a silent teaching partner. When children know where materials are and how to put them away, the teacher can do less "housekeeping" and have more time for interacting with students. When students have access to resources and references for working independently, the teacher can work intensively with small groups. When the teacher has planned for personal storage and traffic patterns, less time is spent mediating conflicts. When materials reinforce the curriculum, provide practice, and nurture creativity, it's almost like the teacher has an extra pair of hands. A rich learning environment invites students into the world of learning and tells them that it is a worthwhile place to be and that they are valued there.

The choices teachers make in setting up their classrooms convey both implicit and explicit messages. The explicit messages are clear to us and we consciously try to make them clear to students, too. Messages might address how students are expected to behave in the classroom and what they are expected to learn. Implicit messages, sometimes called the "hidden curriculum," come through to students just as clearly, but they are often not consciously planned. These implicit messages are too important to leave to chance. Principal Jeanne Villafuerte feels that the hallways and classrooms at West Portal School set the tone for high academic expectations. Fifth-grade teacher Kate Hayes comments:

> My classroom is colorful and full of student work reflecting our curriculum. My students feel a sense of ownership of our classroom and know that Room 16 is not just my classroom, but OUR classroom. They help me keep the room clean and organized and take pride in it.

A sense of welcome and belonging and an invitation into the curriculum can be silently and intentionally communicated to students through features of the physical environment.

Convey a Sense of Welcome and Belonging

Each classroom is unique, reflecting the teacher's and students' interests and personalities for that school year. The most beautifully organized and equipped classroom feels impersonal if it is devoid of the imprint of its inhabitants.

Display Students' Names, Photos, and Work

Displaying students' names, photos, and work prominently throughout the room underscores their ownership of the space. Photos can be brought in by the children, taken by the teacher, or obtained from school pictures. They can be photocopied and used in numerous ways, such as on name cards, labels, and published writing and on graphs. Kindergarten teachers Cathy McNamara and Mary Yuen post their students' photos and first names on the appropriate letter of the alphabet to create a personalized picture cue for the symbol.

Using students' names is one of the most powerful ways to personalize the classroom. In McNamara and Yuen's kindergarten, names are visible all over the room—on birthday charts, on job charts, on sign-up sheets for the author's chair, on schedules for sharing or small-group work, on cubbies, on journals and folders, on the alphabet, and on word-work lists (What begins with___? Which words have the___sound?).

Fill the Classroom with Materials Reflecting Many Cultures

Classrooms can be filled with authentic materials that reflect the students' cultures and world cultures. This helps students take pride in their own background while learning about and appreciating the backgrounds of others. Although celebrating holidays, festivals, and special months is an important way to acknowledge and celebrate cultures, children's exposure to other cultures should be full time and not limited to special events. Teachers can fill the classroom with books and posters that portray a range of racial and ethnic groups, age groups, and literary and artistic traditions, and they can give students opportunities to hear music and stories, see written language, enjoy folk art and textiles, use cooking utensils, smell and taste foods, and experience themselves as citizens of the world. Kindergarten teacher Keiko Chew often plays taped instrumental music from diverse cultures softly while she reads to her class. Teachers can promote sensitivity to people with varying abilities and lifestyles, for example, by modifying a traditional family tree to include all kinds of families.

Families sometimes have cultural artifacts that they are willing to lend the class. Family members can be invited to present such items to the class and then the artifacts can be displayed in the classroom. Karen Freitas' first-/second-grade class calls this display their "multicultural museum." Some teachers encourage students to bring in artifacts when it's their turn to be student of the week.

Reflect Students' Home Languages

The classrooms we visited reflect student's home languages. Printed materials that reflect home languages include labels on food cans in a kindergarten house area, word cards in the writing area, and displays of student's spontaneous writing. Classes play and sing music from home cultures. In a bilingual classroom, materials on shelves can be labeled in the home language as well as English. When labels are in two languages, it is helpful to the emergent reader to designate a particular color for each language. Parents also feel welcomed in the classroom when it's clear that their home languages are appreciated.

Some teachers gather greetings in the many languages of their students by asking families or other native speakers for the correct, most commonly used term for "hello." In Fareeda Christ's classroom, these words are posted on the bulletin board that is the focus for class meetings. Some classes have learned to count in languages other than English and practice together as a whole group. To acknowledge the languages spoken by the children in the class, Mary Ostrom's third grade created a graph using data about the number and names of the languages they speak.

Invite Students into the Curriculum

On the first day of the year, bulletin boards are freshly papered but blank, awaiting decoration by the new cast of players who will occupy the classroom. Teachers can use purchased charts and decorations, but having students make them increases their meaning and usefulness. Students can write captions for displays, help decide what goes up, and use displays in learning activities.

Figure 3–1. The social studies area and display are labeled in both English and Tagalog, the students' home language.

Figure 3–2. The science table includes a variety of materials for a study of silkworms such as informational books, story books and poems, observation journals, photos, tools, and live specimens.

Create Displays That Are a Learning Resource

Through displays that invite students into the curriculum, a learner-centered environment virtually shouts out the topics, concepts, and skills the class is working on. A classroom "explorer's post" might have a collection of artifacts that introduces a social studies topic. A science table might have a collection of nature specimens that children can handle and observe as part of a science unit. A special shelf might feature a collection of books and magazines on the current curricular theme.

Students' work is displayed throughout classroom interest areas, which recognizes their efforts and provides models to inspire other students. For example, student authors' work is posted in the writing area and student book reviews draw children into the classroom library. Displaying surveys of students' interests and experiences taken during math time or as part of social studies creates a feeling of community.

Displays are most effective when students can use them for learning. Resources such as word banks where students can check the spelling of words they want to write, problem-solving charts that students have brainstormed, and directions for various routines allow children to develop self-sufficiency in their learning. Students can help one another by directing classmates' attention to posted materials. Finally, displays help students learn that print has meaning and personal usefulness. Exciting invitations into the curriculum both challenge and welcome students, saying "You are a part of this" and "Don't you want to find out more about this?"

Designate Areas of the Room That Relate to the Curriculum

A classroom that uses student investigation, projects, and student-initiated activity needs to have clearly defined areas where students can find the materials they need and have space to work. Clear organization and labeling those areas with easy-to-read signs make the room a public space that any child or adult can enter and find their way around. A well-organized classroom is no longer the private domain of the teacher, but rather a living space for learners.

Interest areas are clearly defined spaces that hold collections of related materials. These areas are used in addition to "centers," which might be set up just for the duration of a particular activity period. Interest areas contain materials and tools for carrying out tasks of various types.

Some commonly used interest areas are class library, writing area, math area, science area, and art area. Some classrooms have a computer area and a puppet area or other area for staging performances and drama. Kindergarten classrooms have a playhouse area. Classrooms with older students might have a games and puzzles area and a research area with reference materials. Some areas might have materials that are used in different ways, such as a tactile area for young children with a water table filled alternately with water, sand, birdseed, or other pourable, measurable substances. Inviting mini-areas can be set up in a little nook or cranny within a larger area. A word-work area with magnetic letters and word cards works well in a tiny space, as does a listening area with story tapes. Teachers can create temporary special areas to support a curriculum objective or topic, such as a measuring area stocked with measuring tools, a class store or bank, a cooking area, or an area with artifacts and books that reflect the theme of a social studies unit.

Fareeda Christ describes the environment in her third-grade classroom:

I remember feeling tremendously overwhelmed at the prospect of redesigning my room...But now that it is done, I can't imagine functioning any other way. All math materials, including manipulatives, books, games, and activities to further explore concepts are easily located in the math area. Atlases, globes, geography games, reference books, and books on various cultures are organized in the social studies area.

Figure 3–3. A student works with a portable word wall.

Magnifying glasses, science tools, science books, and the latest experiments are either on display or are available here to explore further at the science area.

I take greatest pride in my library, which, through many sources, has grown substantially over the past few years. A wide variety of books are leveled and organized in baskets, ranging from very easy to hard chapter books. Organizing the classroom this way has made teaching and learning easier. Students have access to all materials when doing projects. The tremendous amount of books supports our goal of literacy for all, while they are easy for the children to keep organized (with stickers on books matching stickers on baskets).

In kindergarten and first grade, teachers set up distinct areas separated by long, low shelves. This creates cozy corners and helps children to focus on their work. Each area contains related supplies, which cuts down on the need for students to roam around the classroom gathering supplies.

As students grow bigger and require larger furniture, classroom space shrinks and it sometimes becomes impossible to have distinct areas, as well as enough seating and space for students to move around the classroom. Some whole-group activities may require that all students be able to see an overhead or pocket chart while seated at their tables. Teachers of older children often designate interest areas by using shelves around the periphery of the room. Students' tables or desk groupings are in the middle of the room and can be used as work tables for the nearest interest area.

Organize Common Space and Materials

Space can be pleasing and logical or chaotic and disorienting. It can make us feel welcome or unwanted, graceful or awkward. The way a space is organized can facilitate the completion of our daily tasks, or it can hinder productivity. In a learner-centered approach, classrooms are public spaces that are arranged to support the work of all the members of the classroom community.

Space and time are in short supply in the typical classroom, and teachers always dream of what they could do if they had more. Just as we try to use every minute of the day, we can use every inch in the classroom to further students' school experience. A classroom arrangement that facilitates movement and collaboration and an absence of clutter give optimal support to young learners.

Create a Central Meeting Area

The central meeting area is important to creating a feeling of class community. This is usually a carpeted open space that is large enough for all the members of the classroom to gather in for whole-group activities. Kathy Rosebrock emphasizes the importance of creating space for a circle without crowding. Some teachers

Figure 3–4. The central meeting area in a classroom provides a welcoming space large enough for all to gather.

maximize space by creating an "upper deck" of milk crates or chairs around the edge of the meeting area so that students can sit in two concentric rings.

Other teachers have found that having delineated "seats" on the rug helps children find a place. These "seats" could be spots marked with tape or squares in the pattern of a patchwork rug that's made from rug samples. The central meeting area can be used throughout the day for small-group or individual work. Many teachers have a one-minute routine for moving tables or desks aside to make room for whole-class meetings.

Arrange Furniture to Facilitate Collaboration

Furniture needs to be arranged to facilitate movement and collaboration. With large classes, it can seem like the students and the furniture barely fit in the room. More space for students can be claimed by eliminating extraneous furniture and storage items. Some teachers find that pushing their desk to the wall gives them enough room to create an additional interest area. Other teachers replace their desk with a shelf or rolling cart for materials they need to have within reach. The ultimate space saver, created by San Francisco teacher Kelly Scott, is to organize items on the wall using hanging clipboards for important papers and forms and mounted plastic units with little drawers for stationery supplies.

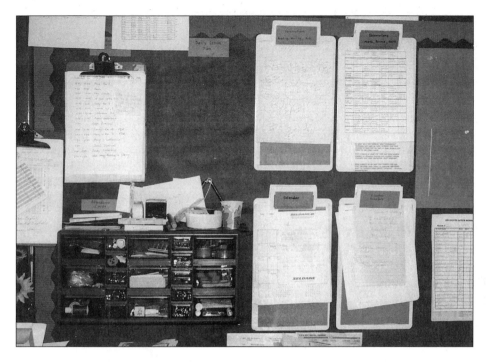

Figure 3–5. Creating a "teacher's desk" on the wall frees up floor space for student use and helps to organize materials.

Tables are an ideal substitute for individual desks because more students can be accommodated in the same amount of space. Using tables means that students must have another space to store items they would have kept in their desks. Teachers find that when materials are accessible in the classroom, students don't need to have individual sets of supplies. Students' ongoing work can be organized in standing files. Books that students are reading independently can be kept in baskets. Kathy Rosebrock uses "book pots," magazine files labeled with each student's name, to hold books for independent reading. Francisco Hernandez has students bring cereal boxes from home, then cuts them at an angle to create standing files that get decorated and labeled with each child's name. Suzanne Vradelis has students keep their books for independent reading in large resealable bags. In her classroom, reference and text materials are stored in the related interest area and distributed as needed. Some teachers put a basket in the middle of each table, stocked with pencils, scissors, erasers, and other supplies for the table group. Elzaida Alcaide takes advantage of these baskets by posting "unknown word strategies" on the sides of baskets so she can refer to them while conferencing with students.

Avoid Classroom Clutter

Clutter is often a result of the volume of student activity in the classroom. Students can help to organize their papers and clean up after activities if they are given a system and routine for doing so. Hanging folders for various subject matter give students a place to easily file and later find their papers. These folders can be kept in a small box in the related interest area (writing folders in the writing area, book logs in the class library, etc.). Some teachers use alphabetized accordion folders for students to file their homework in as they come in each morning. Students are always willing to volunteer to file papers or library books.

Provide a Wide Selection of Materials

Materials work hard in the learner-centered classroom, helping the teacher provide a vast array of experiences in all areas of the curriculum. A well-stocked classroom can engage children in one area of the room while the teacher works with a small group in another area.

With a shortage of funding, teachers must be very resourceful in order to provide their students with a rich selection of materials. Many items in classrooms are recycled, found, purchased at garage sales, or homemade. This does not mean, however, that they are in disrepair. Materials in good condition give a silent message to students: We care for you and therefore we care about the materials we provide for you.

If you ask a craftsperson about her workshop, she is likely to invite you into a physical space, point out with pride the organization of tools and materials, and show you her latest work. This sense of ownership and pride of place can exist for both students and teachers in a learner-centered classroom.

4

A Sense of Belonging

Elementary students actively construct their understanding of the role of "student" and how they fit into that role. Negative images affect their view of school and of themselves as learners. The way students experience the classroom is very much determined by the kinds of peer relationships that prevail. Classrooms can be competitive or judgmental due to student attitudes, with students holding back from expressing their opinions or trying new things because they are not sure how they will be received. No amount of kindness or well-meaning on the teacher's part can overcome a hostile peer environment. The way a teacher guides social relationships within the classroom is important in creating a positive climate for learning.

Promote Positive Relationships Between Students

The beginning of the year is a critical time for focusing on social relationships in the classroom. Teachers can use opening-week assignments that showcase students as individuals and cultivate their respect for one another through read-alouds, shared reading, literature and writing topics, interviews and math surveys, science that uses the local environment, and cultural geography lessons on where students' families came from. Throughout the year, traditions continue the process of building mutual respect.

The first several weeks of the school year are a critical time for community building. As sixth-grade teacher Laurie Roberts reflects,

> This is the twenty-first century and it is imperative that we all work together toward common goals. This is a constant theme in my classroom. Students who are usually unmotivated will do their work for the sake of the group's success, and students who generally keep to themselves and don't like others have learned what coming

to one another's aid means. My advice to teachers who want to create a better classroom environment is this: Build a strong classroom community on the first day of school. Don't stop there! Continue throughout the year with group activities and class meetings.

Jeanne Villafuerte, principal of West Portal School, makes use of a tradition that she learned from *Teaching Tolerance* magazine. When a child has done something positive, the teacher gives him a flower to hold while talking about what he has done. The teacher also places a flower on a tree in the classroom when a child has done something kind.

Principal Terry Edeli writes home to parents:

The elementary school teachers have chosen Valentines as a way to highlight among the children their interconnectedness and the impact their actions and comments can have on each other. In class, teachers are exploring grace and courtesy, friendship and relationship. We are asking children to take guidance from Ralph Waldo Emerson: "The way to have a friend is to be one." For homework this week, children have been asked to create a Valentine card for each child in the class that includes a thoughtful written statement that acknowledges a special attribute or actions. Such acknowledgement goes a long way towards building more confident youngsters and thus a stronger student community.

After reading a book about friendship in Cheryl Nelson's classroom, students made a bulletin board illustrating "ways to say 'I Like You'": "Will you play kickball with me?" "Here's a hug." "I'd like you to come over to my house." James Wade provides his kindergarten with a basket of laminated "hug slips." Students can take one at any time and present it to another child to get a hug, giving them a powerful way to take care of one another nonverbally.

A "student of the week" tradition cultivates respect for each student in the classroom. In Wendy Smithers' class, student names are put into balloons and students pop one balloon each Friday to determine the next "star." In Beth Coy's kindergarten, the student of the week brings a favorite book and photos to share. Parents are invited to attend on Monday, when the class interviews the student of the week and asks parents such questions as "What do you like to do with your child?" and "What was your first thought when you saw your child for the first time?" Students write up the interview and post it on the bulletin board with photos, then make it into a book to take home at the end of the week. Kathy Rosebrock's first graders interview the "big cheese" (student of the week) every Friday, taking dictation on a chart that they decorate for the "big cheese" to take home. Liz Patterson eats lunch with her fifth grade's V.I.P. one day during the week: "I bring the dessert. It is a wonderful way to check in, make strong personal connections, and learn new information about each student.

Suzanne Vradelis shares her procedures for student of the week:

Student-of-the-Week Procedures

Preinterview:

- Brainstorming period: Use a chart of questions that were collected before, add new questions, and give a quiet minute for each child to think of two or three questions.
- Give reminders about respectful listening.

Interview:

- Have students share a special, sentimental object if they brought one. Classmates ask "Where did you get it?" "Why is it special?" "How long have you had it?"
- Allow the student of the week to call on people only if the timing doesn't drag. If it does, the teacher calls on children, making sure everyone contributes a question before anyone gets a second turn.
- Interject some hot-button questions to perk things up: What's the biggest trouble you ever got into? What's the worst thing your brother or sister ever did to you? Did you ever have a serious injury, like broken bones? Stitches? What's the funniest thing that ever happened to you? Scariest? Best? Worst?
- Call on children who haven't asked a question, and if they are not ready, say, "I'll come back to you in a minute. Have a question ready."
- Have a child tally how many questions are asked on the border of a piece of paper telling the kids only one question each. This can encourage thoughtful questioning and discourage students who dominate.
- Students need to listen very carefully to make sure they don't repeat a question.
- Teacher can record on organized chart paper (webbing topics like family, favorites, wishes, etc.) during the interview or during the recall.

Recall:

- The teacher asks, "What do you remember about the student of the week?" Students recall facts that they heard. The teacher calls on students to remember something (not necessarily the ones with their hands up). If a student draws a blank, prompt him by giving hints: What do you remember about her family? What did she say about. . .?
- Recall should go very fast. If someone kept tally of all the questions, they can tally how many facts were remembered: Twenty questions equals twenty facts remembered.
- Students need to listen very carefully to make sure they don't repeat a recalled fact.
- Finish with a quick round of "___ and I are alike because we both. . ." started by the teacher.

Writing:

- Take a few quick minutes to remind students that a good student-of-the-week paper should include the following. Read some finished papers from another week if there's time.

    1. An introductory paragraph telling who the student of the week is.
    2. One or two additional well-organized paragraphs.
    3. A complete outlined and colored drawing that illustrates the paper.
    4. The student's best effort on spelling, punctuation, etc. The teacher can say, "Read it first to yourself, then to a friend to help correct."

- Other elements can be added to the paper as the year progresses: quotations, vocabulary development, author's voice, etc. These elements can be taught in mini-lessons to small groups of students while others are writing.

Sharing:

- The student of the week collects finished papers and checks authors off as they are turned in.
- Read some finished papers to the class if there's time.

Suzanne Vradelis' students brainstormed questions for their student of the week:

- If you had a thousand dollars what would you buy?
- What are your favorite foods?
- What do you like to do in school?
- Where is your family from originally?
- Do you have a brother or sister and what do you like to do together?
- Who else is in your family?
- What are your favorite sports? Do you play any sports?
- What do you think you will be when you grow up?
- What do you do in the summer?
- What are your favorite outside games?
- If you could go anywhere you wanted, where would you go?
- What are the best parts of your life?
- What are you good at and what do you need help with?
- What are your hobbies?
- Where do you live? What is your street like?
- If you could be any animal, what would you be and why?
- If you could be any famous person, who would you be and why?
- What do you like to eat?

- What are your favorite holidays and why?
- Do you have any pets?

Bee Medders asks her kindergarten class to give the student of the week a "warm fuzzy" by using interactive writing to describe qualities they admire about the student. The class as a group writes a sentence about the student. The following week, that sentence and the student's "me doll," a paper doll he made that looks like himself, get made into a poster that stays hung up all year long and serves as a word bank for other class writing. Virtually every teacher we have worked with uses some form of student of the week to build respect and understanding among students.

Fifth-grade students Sonya Chemouni Bach and Tess McNamara describe their school's person-of-the-week tradition in a handbook their class wrote for incoming students:

> In first through fifth grade we have something called Person of the Week. Person of the Week is when one person gets randomly picked to be somebody called Person of the Week. The Person of the Week brings in pictures of themselves and their family and shares them on the following Monday. They usually have a stuffy to take home over the weekend and through the whole week.
>
> In second grade it is a bear called Coco who has a suitcase full of fun clothes. In third grade it is also a bear called Oscar who also has a suitcase of belongings. In fourth grade any kid who wants to can bring in a stuffy and the whole class votes on one of them to use. In fifth grade we have a frog named George, and one that someone brought in called Cheese Boy.
>
> In third grade you have to write something you like about the Person of the Week and draw a picture. For example you could say, "To ___, I like you because you're adventurous, playful and kind. From, ___." The Person of the Week in second and third grade has a journal to write what they did with Oscar or Coco throughout the week.
>
> In fourth grade and second grade you don't have to do anything if you're not Person of the Week. In fifth grade you have to think of a question to ask the Person of the Week, ask them, write down what they say, and draw a picture (personally I think that fifth grade has the best and most fun activities for Person of the Week).

The schoolyard can be a frightening place when older students look down on younger students. Schools that focus on building community promote respect across grade levels. West Portal School has a buddies program—for example, first and fourth graders are buddies. Buddy groups meet once a week to read books, make cards, work on an art project, or take field trips together. At Lawton School, Dan Sobel's fourth-grade students work with Lonnie Lebins' first-grade students. The "big buddies" and "little buddies" trace each other on butcher paper and draw in the clothes they typically wear to make life-size buddy replicas that are displayed in pairs in the school halls.

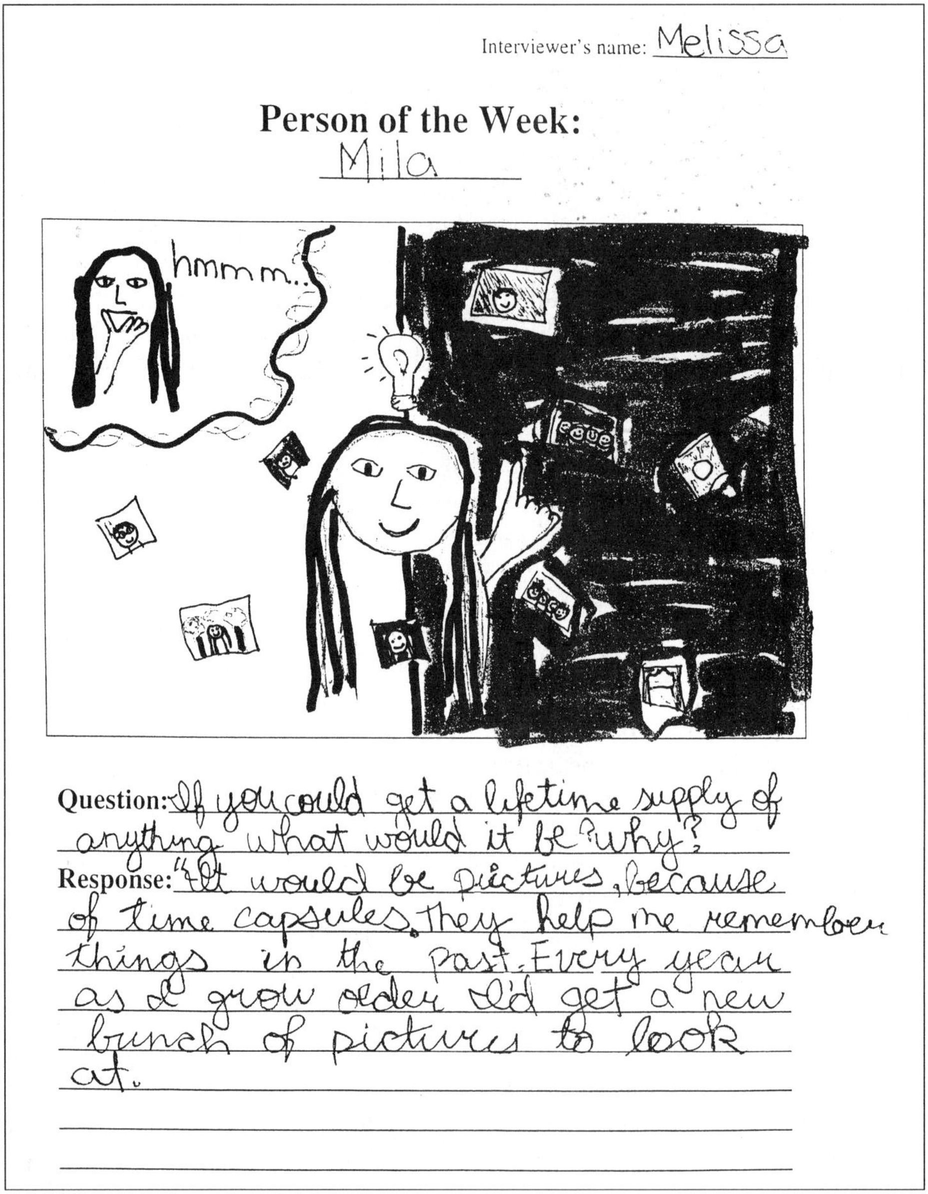

Interviewer's name: Melissa

Person of the Week:
Mila

Question: If you could get a lifetime supply of anything what would it be? why?

Response: "It would be pictures, because of time capsules. They help me remember things in the past. Every year as I grow older I'd get a new bunch of pictures to look at.

Figure 4–1. Fifth-grader Melissa interviews Mila, the "Person of the Week," and illustrates her entry into a class book for Mila to keep.

At the San Francisco School, "school families" consist of one child from each grade. The families stay together from year to year, and siblings are put in the same school family. Families meet for half an hour every five to six weeks to work on a project. The eighth grade has responsibility for the group. When construction was underway in the schoolyard, the eighth graders toured the site, then took their families on tours to point out hazards. When the school assembled to hear about the Columbine tragedy, students sat with their families and older students talked to younger students about how they would be safe and cared for. As principal Terry Edeli explains, "What's exciting is the bonds that it builds cross-age. Without school families, it would be difficult to do."

Cultivate Respect for Differences as Well as Similarities

Over eight weeks, fourth-grade teacher Solveig Dimon and her students read and discussed Dr. Mel Levine's book *All Kinds of Minds*, written to introduce children to different learning styles through stories. Dimon and learning specialist Carla Bach taught the unit together, using Levine's book as core reading. Students developed a better understanding of their own learning styles and approaches to learning and developed empathy for those who have a hard time learning in some areas of the curriculum. The unit also helped students be conscious of what study methods work best for them. Dimon offers students study questions to prepare for social studies tests. Students try different approaches to memorizing key facts, using pneumonic devices and three-by-five-inch cards and making up chants or raps.

By capitalizing on classroom diversity, teachers can cultivate students' respect for and interest in the differences and similarities among people. Young children can understand that everyone has a home, although everyone's home is different. Teachers can use children's books to inspire interest in differences. The picture book *Everybody Cooks Rice* by Norah Dooley (1991) can be used to talk about how we all eat similar foods but prepare them differently. In this book, a girl looks for her brother at neighbors' homes just before dinnertime. She notices the different ways that each neighbor is cooking rice. Cathy McNamara's and Mary Yuen's classes enjoy having a rice potluck to celebrate this book, with each family bringing in rice prepared their favorite way. Ann Morris' series of photographic picture books on themes such as bread, houses, and hats around the world can also be used to teach about similarities and differences.

Modeling how to be interested rather than fearful about differences helps students learn to interact with children of other backgrounds with comfort and empathy. When teachers and parents are willing to talk about differences in a positive way, they provide a model for students. Sometimes adults are uncomfortable acknowledging differences and try to act like they are "colorblind" and that

---

Festival of Breads

Dear Family,

French Bread, Pita Bread, Tortilla, Naan, Whole Wheat Bread, Bao, Matzo, Injera, Cracker, Bagel, Bolillo, Biscuit, White Bread, Roll, Bread Stick, Pretzel, and ....?????

We are learning about "Breads Around the World." Learning about different breads is very interesting. It is also a wonderful way to get to know about different cultures.

Does your family have a favorite bread? If so, would you like to send some to school for our Bread-Tasting Day next Friday, May 27th? If you plan to send a bread sample please return the sign-up below. Thank you for contributing. The children will enjoy the variety very much.

Sincerely,
Donna Lindsay & Mike Price

— —

Yes, I will send some bread for sampling on Friday.

_____
Name or type of bread

_____   _____
Parent's name   Child's name

Figure 4–2. Families are invited to participate in a "Festival of Breads," a class tasting of breads from their home cultures.

everyone is the same. This can indicate to children a lack of interest in differences and lead them to assume that people's uniqueness is not valued. We know that an internalized feeling of inferiority is extremely damaging, but a false sense of superiority is damaging too. Building self-esteem by creating a false sense of superiority does not help children grow and develop.

It is important to convey to students that each and every one of them is unique, and therefore different. There is no one "right" way to be, nor is there a cultural norm from which others deviate. Each of us seems "different" to those who don't know us.*

Share Control with Students by Making Their Voices Heard

In a community of learners, students' voices need to be heard if teachers are to share control of and responsibility for the classroom community. Regular class meetings build community through discussing topics of common interest. Class meetings have traditionally been used to resolve conflicts, but they can do more to build community and give voice to each child: They can be used to make group decisions (about a party, a field trip, a special project); plan procedures (how to share playground equipment); discuss and plan for upcoming transitions (the student teacher leaving, a substitute arriving); or share feelings about events both happy and sad. Kathy Rosebrock uses class meetings to introduce new materials and activities to her first graders. Class meetings can be formal (held once a week with an agenda) or informal (held as needed when a decision must be made about a change of plans, problem with a procedure, etc.).

Diana Sottile describes how her third-grade students began to run their class meetings:

> By the end of January, all students had had a chance to be Student of the Week. At this time, we generated a list of "responsibilities and privileges" that the Student of the Week would have for the second round. One of the things the students asked for was to run our class meetings. It wasn't my idea! They always seem to come up with the best ideas. And when you allow students to do this, you also learn a lot about where they are developmentally and what their needs are. So, it was settled. The Student of the Week would be responsible for, among

---

* *Teaching Tolerance*, a 64-page, full-color magazine published by the nonprofit Southern Poverty Law Center, is mailed free to educators twice a year. For a subscription, write to Teaching Tolerance, 400 Washington Ave., Montgomery, AL 36104, or fax a request to (334) 264-7310. Free copies of the book *Responding to Hate at School* are also available. Find out more at www.teachingtolerance.org.

other things, running our biweekly class meetings. This means going through the agenda items, facilitating the discussion, and choosing the sharing topic to go around the circle.

I must admit, I didn't think it would work. "They will surely need my guidance," I thought. But much to my delight, at the next class meeting, the Student of the Week proudly got the Agenda and a chair and began to go through the items as the rest of the class sat in a circle on the carpet. One student had a problem to share. When she had stated the problem, Sarah, the Student of the Week, responded, "Would you like to do an 'I-Statement'?"

"Yes," the student responded, and went on to follow the chart on the wall. "Jake, I feel annoyed when you forget to raise your hand to speak, and I want you to stop." Then Sarah pipes in, "Okay, restate the problem, Jake." Jake restates the problem and then Sarah asks, "Do you feel better about it now?"

I sit back in awe. They are repeating the exact words I have been using for months. I am bursting with pride. They don't need me. They understand the process and are listening to each other and sharing their feelings.

Class Meetings are a regular part of our weekly schedule. When I made my plan book, I included two half-hour blocks each week for Class Meetings. This way I don't forget to schedule it every week like I did last year. Last year class meetings slowly disappeared; there was too much else to do, and I didn't make it a priority. But this year, by INKING it into my plan book, it is a regular part of our week. The students know when we will have class meetings, and it's a great way to end the week on Fridays.

Class Meetings are not just a problem-solving time, but a time to bond as a class, listen, laugh, dream, share special treasures, toys and pets, as well as appreciations and compliments. It's a happy time!

What struck me the most is the way that Class Meetings create a shift in the energy of the class at the beginning of the year. Suddenly, students are happy; they also feel ownership of the class and our procedures. I can literally observe the classroom community strengthening. Students know that they will be respected and heard during our class meetings. They know they can make a suggestion about how we do things in class, or what to study. They know that I will consider the suggestion and put it out to the class for discussion. We vote a lot! The process does take time and does require patience on the part of the teacher, but when you let the process proceed at "kid speed," the results are amazing.

Kindergarten students in Glendi Henion-Ul's classroom hold "emergency" class meetings to role-play conflict resolution with puppets or discuss problems that need solving. Students will stop in the middle of projects to convene a meeting if necessary, and take their role in solving problems very seriously. In addition to creating a sense of belonging, class meetings teach children how to build and reach consensus and to function as a microcosm of a democratic society. Kate Hayes comments:

During our class meeting, we begin with some compliments for each other, or "highs and lows" (one good thing/one bad thing). During class meetings, we discuss issues and problems students are having on the playground and how to solve them. During class and group work, students have learned how to discuss issues politely, saying such comments as "I'll have to disagree with you."

Regular class meetings have been shown to have a significant impact on students' feelings of community (Lewis, Schaps, and Watson 1996). Cheryl Nelson's second-grade class talks about values at class meetings:

> Each child had a turn with the "talking stick" and said "I am responsible when. . ." (". . . I take care of my little sister," ". . . I clean my room"). We had a meeting when we talked about put-downs. We concluded that when someone has given you a put-down the best way to "shake it off" is to think of some area where you really excel. So we ended the meeting with a round of "I am really great at. . ." Then we grabbed that idea, held it to our hearts, and kept it there for when we need it.

The school day in a learning community is ripe with opportunities for students to express themselves in large- and small-group settings. Pairing students up gives them a less threatening setting in which to make their voices heard and lets them check out their ideas before sharing with the whole class. Partnering can happen throughout the classroom, giving everyone a chance to participate in a discussion at the same time. To begin partnering, the teacher asks students to turn to the person next to them and discuss the idea at hand. Partnering can be used for writing prompts or as warm-ups to class discussions. It is also useful when many students are anxious to talk and contribute all at once. Sally Kaneko's first-/second-grade class uses "teddy bear buddies" who take "my turn/your turn." When Bee Medders calls on a kindergartner, she says to the class, "It's Mary's turn to speak. Everyone listen." To give everyone an opportunity to express their ideas, she often asks students to turn to a partner and share.

Assigning competence is another way to help children form positive images of one another. In her observations of students working in cooperative groups, Elizabeth Cohen (1994) found a hierarchy in which "high-status" students take the lead and the contributions of "low-status" students are ignored. Cohen recommends a "status treatment" to counteract the effects of social status on student participation and learning. In the status treatment, teachers explicitly and publicly speak about the strengths and talents of specific children and about how that child's abilities can contribute to the task at hand. For example, a teacher might say to the whole group, "When you get to the computation part of the project, please check with Marcos. He is really good with numbers." Teachers also speak frequently about the multiple abilities needed to carry out group tasks and design activities that require a variety of expertise. This technique helps students serve as resources to each another. Cohen cautions that these exchanges must be authentic.

Jenette Sparks developed a "talking mural" that hangs in the hallway outside her first-grade classroom. The mural showcases students' responses to a question ("Who is in your family?" "What will you do during summer vacation?") in speech bubbles next to their self-portraits. The questions and responses, which say "this is who we are," get changed periodically. A "talking mural" is a visual way to make students' voices "heard."

Teach Social Skills, Including Sharing Divergent Opinions

In the upper grades in particular, peer influence is an important social issue. Developmentally, students in these grades can explore differing viewpoints and develop more than one solution for a problem or resolution to an issue. Teachers can establish a classroom climate that values and welcomes a variety of viewpoints. As students move on to middle school, such modeling can help them take a stand on the difficult issues adolescents face. Teachers can help students learn to voice their opinions in a number of ways:

- In small groups, ask students to brainstorm their ideas about an issue or problem confronting the class. One student then reports for each group, and ideas can be listed by the teacher or another student.
- Ask students to take a stand on a question.
- Ask students, "Can you add anything to that?"
- In class meetings or discussions, give a list of suggestions or questions that elicit opinions ("How do you feel about...?") Ask students to use their thumbs to give their opinions quickly:
    Thumbs up—agree
    Thumbs down—disagree
    Thumbs sideways—no opinion or pass
- Draw an imaginary line in the classroom and tell the class it is a "continuum." Identify the ends as "strongly agree" and "strongly disagree" and the middle as the place for those who have no opinion, choose to pass, or consider themselves to be "in the middle of the road." Ask questions and have students to place themselves along the continuum according to their answer (Gibbs 1995).
- In small groups, tell students you will be asking them to make some choices. Tell them to write down the three choices you dictate. Ask them to think about the choices and number them 1, 2, and 3 in order of preference. Ask the groups to discuss their choices among themselves. What did they choose? Why? Was the decision easy or hard? This technique can then be used in class decision making (Gibbs 1995).

- Encourage debate by having individuals give contrasting opinions or having teams take sides. Have each side take the other side's perspective into account before the debate so they'll be able to give considered responses.
- Use literature to validate differing points of view. Students can respond to current events or give their opinion of a book or movie. Use language that values a variety of responses: "Jake has an interesting point here. . ."
- Encourage public speaking by having students write up their opinions in writer's workshop or social studies, then inviting them to address the class or another group on an issue of concern. Have students give their name, age, or grade, and a brief personal description as an introduction to their piece.
- Model how to say "no" by having students role-play peer-pressure situations and brainstorm responses, including what language they might use to give themselves space. Ask each student to choose a phrase and visualize themselves using it:

    "Let me think about it."

    "That's an interesting idea."

    "That doesn't work for me right now."

    "Sounds like fun, but. . ."

    "I'm outta here."

Ann Park trains her fifth-grade students to use hand signals she has learned from Project SEED®, a model mathematics education program, to express their opinions silently at any time. Park finds that using silent signals is less intimidating for students than speaking is, and students don't feel as open to rejection when they use signals to express their opinions. The Project SEED® hand signals include these:

Agreement: Pump both hands in the air with hands in a loose fist to indicate "I agree."

Disagreement: Wave both hands crossing back and forth in front of you, palms down, to indicate "I disagree."

Partial agreement: Make the agreement signal with one arm and the disagreement signal with the other arm.

Answers: Use fingers to indicate numbers, letters, and other symbols.

Uncertainty: Shrug shoulders and hold palms up and out to side, arms bent, to indicate "I don't know" or "I'm not sure."

Questions: Bend one arm into a hook and use the other fist to make a dot to indicate "I have a question."

Silent applause: Make a clapping motion with your hands but stop before they touch.

I had the same answer: Pat yourself on the back.

Some teachers use writing, as well as whole-group activities, as a way for students to register their views. The teacher invites students to write complaints in a journal as problems occur. Complaints can be used as class meeting agenda items and to generate solutions for students to try. Journals can be used to talk about things that are not working in the classroom. Students who need time to cool off or who feel that they have been treated unfairly can be asked to write about it in a letter to the teacher or another student, or in a journal or learning log. Occasionally the teacher may ask a student's permission to read her letter to the class or a small group in order to sensitize them about a particular issue.

Posting a blank agenda for class meetings gives teachers and students a place to write topics that have not been brought to closure or that warrant further discussion. Suzanne Vradelis makes use of a "bug box," the problem-solving equivalent of the old-fashioned suggestion box. Students write things that are bugging them on a slip of paper and put it in the box. These notes can go on a list of unfinished business, become the basis of a conference with a student or pair of students, or be an invitation to look at a curricular issue.

Bug Box
- Use a medium-sized box with a slit in the top.
- Have students write their beefs, complaints, and issues with other students on small pieces of paper and put their own names on the slips, but *not* write the names of who they are complaining about.

  > For example: "I don't like when kids keep yelling at me to stop shaking the table when I'm not." Andrea

- Two to three times a month, sit in a circle and go through the bug box, with the teacher reading the notes aloud and leaving off the names. Problem-solve or role-play as a group about how each issue might be resolved.

Students may want to designate a particular area of the room for solving problems between students. The teacher can post problem-solving guidelines there and have students use a log or a simple form to sum up the problem and the recommended solution.

Student Emily Herman describes how her class came up with their peace process:

> The Peace Process is a process for resolving our problems. It started in fourth grade, when we got into many fights and we didn't know how to resolve them. We went through a long process of talking about problems and finding different ways to solve them. We started by making suggestions of what we should do to resolve things. In

fifth grade we thought of "The Peace Process," in which there is a mediator who helps to go through the Peace Process and won't take sides. We (the fifth-grade class) thought of ground rules that everyone has to remember and respect when you're going through the steps in the process.

They came up with these steps:

1. Have a cool-down period if needed.
2. Have each person tells their side of the story.
3. Check in with the mediator and ask for more information if you still don't understand.
4. Have each person share what they need to feel better.
5. Find a solution that addresses each person's needs.
6. If your agreement isn't working, check in with the other person.

The students taught the process to the other grades, being careful to choose language the first and second graders would understand and be able to use. Second graders in Nameta Tolia-Henbest's classroom paired up with buddies, role-played how to solve a conflict, and recorded their process. In this process, students role-play a conflict with their partner, going through four steps to resolve it:

1. Say what happened.
2. Say how you feel.
3. Say what you need.
4. Come up with a solution.

At Bessie Carmichael School in downtown San Francisco, principal Amy Talisman holds a Yellow Ribbon Week when classes focus on peace and the nonviolent resolution of problems. Community speakers, including an ex–gang member who changed his life, address the students. The whole school gathers to make this pledge:

> As part of my community and Bessie Carmichael School,
> I will choose to be a caring and kind person.
> I will respect others' belongings.
> I will refrain from making fun of others.
> I will encourage others to do the same.
> I will do my part to make my community a safe place.
> I will eliminate bad words from my language.
> I will choose words and actions that make others feel good.
> I will use words to settle arguments.
> I realize anger and violence doesn't solve problems. . . it
> creates them.
> I will be a Peacemaker.

Figure 4–3. Nika and Joaquin resolve a problem using their schools' "Peace Process."

Give Students Ways to Take a Break

Colombe Allen, an Oakland, California, teacher and teacher educator, encourages teachers to explicitly teach social skills such as respect, responsibility, kindness, and caring. She advocates focusing on what social skills are needed rather than on behavior. Teachers can use class meetings to role-play social skills and post a list of the skills that have been discussed. Teachers need to be on the lookout for opportunities to ask, "How could this have gone differently?"

There are moments in every classroom when the teacher or students need to take a break, reflect on what is happening, and make a change. For teachers, this need is often related to something in the curriculum that is not working, student actions or comments that the teacher needs to reflect on, inappropriate classroom practices, or stresses outside of the classroom. But for teachers, like other performers, the show must go on, even when we would prefer some time alone.

Students need to take a break for many of the same reasons teachers do. If a teacher inadvertently gives inappropriate assignments that are culturally insensitive, or if students feel incompetent, students may act out in response or simply not know what to do or how to participate. Interactions with other students or outside stresses can also contribute to students acting out.

Teachers need to assert their authority and put an immediate stop to actions that show disrespect or undermine the learning community. Some new teachers hold back from asserting their authority for fear they will not earn the students' respect, often producing the opposite effect.

Here are some ways teachers can call for a break while maintaining students' dignity and contributing to their reflection:

- Redirect, remind, and don't fuss.
- Stop the action. Ask the group to freeze for a moment, and describe what is going on. See if members of the group need to take a break and find a solution. If they do, hold a quick class meeting or call for a partner chat.
- In the beginning of the year, if students are disruptive in group situations, tell them to return to their desks and take out some work. Let them know they can try again later but that they must take time to think for a few minutes.
- If a student is losing it, get close to her, speak in a quiet voice, and ask if she needs a break. Repeat your behavioral expectations softly, sternly, and with kindness.
- Have a social conference with a student and together find a way for the student to take a break when he needs it. For some students this could mean sitting somewhere quietly; for others it could mean going to another room. Work out a signal or other way to communicate that the child needs a break.

- When you start to feel angry, write to the students on an overhead transparency or have a written conversation with an individual student. This has a quieting effect on everyone in the classroom.
- Ask students to return to their seats and write or draw about what they see going on.
- When you are really angry with a student, let her know what makes you angry and add, "I wouldn't want to see you treated that way."
- If a student loses it, or you lose it with a student, don't end the day without talking it through.
- If a student behaves inappropriately, turn to him and say, "We need your help."
- Designate a place in the room students can retreat to when they need a break. Provide a journal they can write or draw in to express their feelings.

The way students and teachers perceive and exercise self-control and external control in the classroom can be viewed along a two-dimensional continuum.

Where external control is high, students' self-control is limited. As external control decreases, self-control increases. This view of classroom management sees external control as a situationally-specific tool rather than as the whole of classroom management. External control can be used on a contingency basis in specific situations, rather than being engraved in stone for the whole year or over generalized. When there is rapport among members of a class; when the learning content is made interesting, meaningful, and accessible to students; and when the learning processes employed are appropriate and understandable, few external controls are necessary. However, when these practices are inadequate or missing altogether, external controls are usually necessary for maintaining order and productivity in the classroom.

Each teacher, with each year's class, needs to intervene to refocus student behavior. How does the classroom teacher measure the effects of this intervention? Curwin and Mendler (1988) offer some concrete ways to judge whether disciplinary actions are accomplishing the goal of self-control:

- What happens to the student ten minutes after an intervention? Is he angry? Is he back to the lesson? Do you see signs of passive-aggressive behavior? Is he participating?
- What happens to the student the next day?
- What happens to the student a week later?
- What happens to student motivation? Does energy for learning increase or decrease? (Good discipline plans enhance student motivation, not erode it.)
- What happens to the student's dignity? Is it attacked? Is it maintained? Is it enhanced?

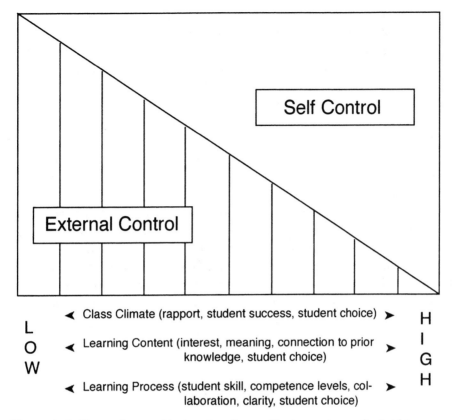

Figure 4–4. External control is situationally specific, increasing or diminishing according to the level of positive climate, compelling content, and engaging learning processes at work in the classroom.

- How is the student's locus of control affected? Does the student become more internally focused on his own behavior? Does the student become more externally focused? (An internal orientation, when appropriate, leads to responsibility. An external orientation leads to helplessness.)
- What happens to the teacher-student relationship? Is communication improved? Is it weakened? Did the teacher win the battle (get the student to do what you wanted) and lose the war (destroy their delicate relationship)?
- Does the student learn about her behavior in a way that provides increased choices, or does the student learn that she has no choice at all? Choices lead to responsibility.

When students act out, teachers can view it as an act of sanity, a cry for help, and look not only to the student but also to the curriculum for answers. Working with the student and looking at the whole child lets teachers hear the student's concerns, share their own concerns, and work toward solutions that work for both. While some methods of external rewards and punishments result in quick responses from students, they do not necessarily give students the skills that will serve them in the future. In a community of learners, problems are solved through individual conferences, mediation, social contracts, and giving students time to reflect. When facing a problem students think "What can we do about this and how can we help?" rather than "What should we do to him?" A community of learners lets students construct solutions to their own problems. According to Piaget, "moral autonomy appears when the mind regards as necessary an ideal that is independent of all external pressure" (1965).

Having the skills to solve complex problems and being able to work both collaboratively and autonomously is often mentioned as one of the list of qualities needed to be successful in the twenty-first century. In a community of learners, students learn how to solve problems by constructing the solution rather than by being told what to do. The twenty-first century will hold challenges for our students. We aim our classroom practices toward teaching them how to meet those future challenges as well as solve today's problems.

5

Personal Best

When used in discussing classrooms, the word "discipline" is usually thought of in terms of punishments, rewards, or both. When used by those striving for mastery, the word takes on a different meaning: For a musician or craftsperson, "discipline" refers to the thoroughness with which the work is done and the degree of attention that is paid it. The rigor with which a skill is approached comes from an internal drive for accomplishment. Learner-centered teachers strive to develop a classroom where students develop genuine self-discipline that is reflected in how they solve a complex problem or revise a piece of writing,

> It is not so much that a teacher provides a model to imitate. Rather, it is that the teacher can become part of the student's internal dialogue—somebody whose respect he wants, whose standards he wishes to make his own. It is like becoming a speaker of a language one shares with somebody. The language of that interaction becomes a part of oneself, and the standards of style and clarity that one adopts for that interaction become a part of one's own standards. (Bruner 1966, 124)

When we have visited academically rigorous learning communities, we have noticed that the teachers have a particular tone in common. Their communications are clear and direct. Students know that there is control and order in the classroom, and they respond with a respect that comes not from fear, but from knowing that there is an adult they can rely on, that they will be safe in this classroom, and that they will be expected to do their best.

Teachers cannot assume that students already know what they want. Along with bridging a generational divide, teachers must bridge cultural differences in communication styles. In a 1998 interview in *Teaching Tolerance* magazine, Lisa Delpit was asked how white teachers of diverse student groups can assert personal authority without perpetuating what Delpit has named "the culture of power."

I want to talk about it culturally rather than racially. There are young black teachers who were brought up in a nontraditional black culture who are more mainstream in their upbringing and would have problems similar to some white teachers. And there are white teachers so familiar with the culture of the African American children they teach that they produce excellent results.

In asserting personal authority, the key is not to look to change who you are. Instead, there are certain areas one can focus on to seek solutions when problems arise. For example, turning a directive into a question—"Would you like to sit down now?" or "Isn't it time put the scissors away?"—is a polite form of speech that is a mainstream, particularly female, structure. Many kids will not respond to that structure because commands are not couched as questions in their home culture. Rather than asking questions, some teachers need to learn to say, "Put the scissors away" and "Sit down *now*" or "Please sit down now."

Teachers whose students come from home cultures different from their own can seek mentors from the same cultures as their students for help and advice.

Make Learning Explicit

When we watch excellent teachers teach, we are struck by the ways in which they are "transparent" to their students, speaking to the whole class explicitly about skills or strategies they want them to learn, or sitting beside students and pointing out problems as a coach or coworker would. These teachers show students how what they are learning will further the purposes of their lives. Students respond well to being treated with respect, to not being patronized, and to not having the learning process or curriculum made mysterious to them.

When we talk about meeting students where they are, we do not mean that children can't move beyond their current developmental level with a particular skill or concept. To the contrary, by knowing where children fall on a developmental continuum, we can plan activities and interactions to move them on to the next step. For example, when we see that a child is stumbling over the first syllable of big words, we can sit down with him, point out the pattern that we see, and let him know that there are concrete strategies for breaking down big words—strategies that good readers and good spellers use. To paraphrase Frank Smith, we can help students feel that they are members of the literacy club (1988).

Brian Cambourne cautions:

There is a danger that these notions could be interpreted to mean that teachers necessarily have to be milksop approvers of anything and everything any learner produces. This is not so. Teachers' responses must be genuine and if they do not like or approve of a learner's attempt then they are bound to let the learner know. In short, expectations can also have a hard edge to them. Two plus two does not equal five;

Figure 5–1. Second graders illustrate reasons to read as they take ownership of reading for their own purposes.

it is, from a meaning perspective, quite wrong. Similarly, there are conventions of spelling, punctuation, and so on which, while possessing little of the inherent "rightness" or "logic" of mathematics, nevertheless have to be met. These are hard-edged expectations. The necessity of meeting them ought to be clearly and unambiguously communicated to learners. (1988, 60)

Demonstrate Clear Expectations and Clear Criteria

Teachers must be clear about the quality of work they expect. Sharon Blackburn models behaviors that show her first graders how they can meet expectations. Robert Marosi stops his fourth-grade bilingual class as they work in small groups to review a chart hanging in his classroom: "Here it is. Before you can do 'Da Opinion,' you have to gather facts. Without facts, how can you form an opinion about what happened?" Bee Medders describes how she makes expectations clear in her kindergarten:

Early in the year, I talk the children through what is expected. I describe explicitly what the behavior looks like versus using vague words (line up "nicely," sit "properly," do a "good" job). I describe what a good job looks like ("Sam remembered to put his name on his paper. He put his paper in the in-box. He put the markers away."). I try to stay away from judgmental comments. I use praise that reinforces desired behaviors and work habits. I AVOID saying things like "That's perfect." "Make it neater next time." "That's great but clean up your mess." "Look how so and so did it." To foster risk-taking, we say when someone makes a mistake, "It's okay to make mistakes, you can learn from your mistakes."

When teachers have built a community of learners, they are able to exert the personal authority that is needed to truly instruct students and give them access to the knowledge they need to become what they want to be.

Cultivate a Sense of "Personal Best" and Student Responsibility

In addition to being clear about what students need to learn, we must communicate to them our belief in their ability to achieve and turn out higher quality work. We do this by making demands that are challenging but achievable. We also model our perseverance and belief by constantly trying new strategies to reach students. We assume that students will succeed if we can find the right strategy to help them make connections. Students often attribute success to being born smart. We work to dispel that erroneous idea by showing students that we work hard to get smart (Howard 1991) and by recognizing effort.

When five-year-olds bring their work to Keiko Chew, she asks, "Is this your best work?" or "How do you think you could make this better?" Bee Medders' kindergarten class has established and written the class rule "I will do my very best," inspired by *The Little Engine That Could*. In Ann Park's class there is one word that is not allowed: "can't." Kathy Rosebrock reminds her first-grade students what good learners do and has them pat themselves on the back after they do what good readers and writers do.

Principal Jeanne Villafuerte takes a hands-on role in imparting a sense of personal best to the students at her school. Fourth-grade students give Villafuerte copies of their writing once a week. She goes into their classrooms and talks with them about their writing from the standpoint of "I'm the audience." Villafuerte knows the names of each of her five hundred–plus students, and she shares this poem by Wang Zhi-Huan from the T'ang dynasty with them:

> **Climbing Stork Tower**
> The white sun sinks behind the hills.
> The Yellow River rushes to the sea.
> Want to see a thousand miles further?
> Let's climb a little higher!

At Washington School, principal Kaye Burnside challenged her students to collectively read ten thousand pages, promising she would host an all-school read-aloud dressed in her pajamas. A hallway display charted students' progress, and when ten thousand pages were reached, the whole staff joined Burnside in coming to school in pajamas.

At a time when physical education is increasingly being ignored in elementary schools, Lawton School holds a K–8 "Olympics." Each class picks a country to represent, wears the colors of that country, and carries its flag in an opening parade that ends in the formation of five circles. Principal Jolie Wineroth reads the pledge of the Olympic Games. Parents and volunteers participate as students run the fifty-yard dash, throw the shot put, and do other events. The emphasis is put on students' doing their personal best.

At Golden Gate Elementary School, each child has a space, labeled with their name and photo, on the hallway bulletin boards. Some teachers have a "sharing wall" where children can display items they've chosen, or a "wall portfolio" where students periodically post their best work so that their growth can be seen by flipping through the pages they have posted.

An excellent way to help students learn how to do their best work is by involving them in designing rubrics for their work. Third-grade teacher Mary Ostrom asked her students to describe three levels of work in response to a math task: "try harder," "so-so," and "wow." Students discussed what the work would look like at each level and Ostrom posted a chart so students could refer to the descriptors before completing a task to make sure they had met the standard. Other teachers have shared the rubrics used to score work with students as they did an assignment, letting students use the rubric to improve their work before submitting it. Teachers can use the following steps to devise a rubric with students, alone, or with other teachers:

1. Look at actual samples of students' work.
2. Do a "loose sort" into broad levels of achievement.
3. Find strong models (anchors or exemplars) for each level.
4. Discuss the choices for models and be sure that all agree to them.
5. Go back and decide what traits characterize each level of achievement.
6. Write these traits into a rubric, listing them in parallel fashion describing each descending level of achievement in as positive a manner as possible.

To accompany rubrics, teachers need to give students clear criteria for what the outcome or product of a project should be. The criteria must be posted and clearly understood by all students. When learner-centered teachers organize learning experiences into projects, they clearly define what they want students to learn, making criteria clear from the outset. Some teachers have their students use the "three C's" (Kovalik and Olsen 1994) to evaluate products: Is it complete? Is it correct? Is it comprehensive? Students also debrief their group process with the whole class, reporting on what worked well, what problems they had working together, and what they could do differently next time.

Robert Marosi has his class do collages, stipulating that the collages must have "a foreground, a background, and a prominent image." This results in an astounding array of beautifully detailed collages. Students then write the stories connected to their pictures. Marosi leads a class discussion that models the story-writing process and allows students to talk about the "how to's" of writing. This work with writing is based on a rubric of four elements: topic, convention, organization, and style. Marosi describes how he works with students as they write their stories:

> When we do something like this, we study the setting, which has to do with the topic. Style has to do with different things like dialogue, synonyms. With organization we talk about outlines and mappings. For convention we look at spelling, capitals, punctuation.

Marosi wants his students to know "This has to do with improving my writing, and writing has to do with a lot of things—it's not just about spelling." He is very conscious of which students have not yet constructed a personal work ethic, and pointedly intervenes to help them do so.

Figure 5–2. A unit on insects is culminated with oral presentations of students' research on a bug of their choice.

Wendy Smithers challenges her students to use more descriptive words in their writing and speaking: "We record rich vocabulary, 'gems,' by writing the words on a plastic laminate sheet with dry-erase pens. It hangs in the window. Students *really* listen for unusual vocabulary and strive to use descriptive words. It's fun." Fourth-grade teacher Solveig Dimon reads a literature passage with action verbs, then sends her class in small teams to other rooms and to the construction site on campus to think of strong verbs to describe the actions they see. Students report their findings to the class, setting a norm for using strong verbs in their daily writing.

Classroom communities must acknowledge and celebrate students' efforts and incremental progress toward high standards. This is part of recognizing that each learner is on her own path, following her own timetable. Bee Medders' kindergarten has a time called "celebration" when they celebrate a child's writing. The child sits in the author's chair and reads finished or in-progress writing and receives an audience response. Medders reads the child's story, with expression, and comments on two or three points that illustrate what good writers do. Medders comments, "It sets a form of rubric for writing and gives examples of topics students can write about."

Elicit Students' Voices

Karen Ferguson describes how she listened to one student's voice in her second-/third-grade classroom:

> This year I had four students from the class I taught the previous year. Alex was one of these students. He came from Samoa. He said to me, "Mrs. Ferguson, you never teach us about Samoa." I said, "Alex, you're right! This year we'll do Samoa."
>
> We did do Samoa. First, I went to the library and checked out as many books as I could find. There are not a lot of books on Samoa. These books were displayed on a table for Sustained Silent Reading. I also read them a story about anthropologist Margaret Mead, who studied the Samoan culture. I got little booklets on Samoa and made copies for each child. I enlarged these so the print was easier to read. The vocabulary and content were a bit difficult. We did shared reading and I would stop at a word. They would say the next word, so I would know they were following along with me. The children underlined important information or words as I read. When we would go back to review, they only read what was underlined. Volunteers who wanted to be the teacher could go in front of the room and ask questions of the class on this information. This theme was used in journal writing during the week.
>
> I had two Samoan children whose parents were a great help. They brought in real tapa cloth and fabric with tapa designs. Alex also brought in a video of his family showing a Samoan celebration. He told us about the food, music, and dress. When I felt the children were ready, we did writing on Samoa using the writing process. It took about three days. We also did an art project on tapa cloth. This also took a long time. We discussed the designs on Sua and Alex's fabrics. I made copies of the fabric. We spent weeks just drawing these designs.

In many ways, a collective work ethic is learner-driven. Reading books they want to read, writing about their own lives and interests, and inquiring into subjects they are naturally curious about gives students an intrinsic motivation to learn. Learner-centered classrooms work most effectively when attention is paid to developing a collective work ethic as well as the academic curriculum; when expectations are high for student participation as well as for academic accomplishment. When students are asked to develop rubrics and to resubmit work because it is not their personal best, they feel valued as people who can reach high standards. Glendi Henion-Ul describes how she shares control with her kindergarten students:*

> Students have lots of choice during the day, during each activity, about where the units of study are headed or what unit we should start next (What do you want to learn about?). Sometimes we vote about a specific activity (for example, should we go outside and have a short plan-do-review time, or stay in for a long one?). We take

---

* The "plan-do-review" idea Glendi speaks about is from M. Hohmann, B. Banet, and D. Weikart (1978) *Young Children in Action*.

notes about their ideas for making big books and then try to come to consensus. We do a lot of writing down of what students say when talking about whole-class graphs, during important class meetings. They see their name and what they've said. They realize we think it's important because it is posted on the butcher paper for all to see. We talk out the consequences of "majority rules" when there is a big split about something. We talk about compromise and the possibility of first this, then that.

From the first day of school, teachers put in place the climate and practices that allow students not only to construct knowledge, but also to construct ways of working together effectively. When students have many opportunities to have their voices heard, their opinions listened to, and their insights appreciated, they feel valued as community members.

Create Positive Working Conditions

Working conditions that help students achieve their best work are critical to constructing a collective work ethic. A consistent, predictable daily schedule supports the teacher—when students know where they should be, what they should be doing, how much time they have, and what to do next, teachers can spend less time "directing traffic" and more time interacting with students. When students know that their needs for whole-group comradery, opportunities to process with others in small group, and the chance to work independently will be met, they feel safe enough to take the risks inherent in learning.

Provide a Consistent Daily Schedule

Having a consistent daily schedule with a known sequence of events lets students relax and focus on learning. Students need to know how the day will begin, what activities will take place before recess, what they can expect before lunch, etc. Predictability sets up a rhythm that is conducive to productivity. Many learner-centered teachers post the daily routine in the classroom so that everyone can refer to it. Some post the routine on sentence strips in a pocket chart to make it easy to add special and semiweekly activities. Young children's emergent understanding of how to tell time can be supported by placing cards with small clock faces next to each time block on a pocket chart. Referring to the names of the time blocks and comparing the time on the clock-face cards to the real clock helps students learn to tell time.

Some teachers prefer to write an agenda on the blackboard each day with the day's activities. They take time in the morning meeting to go over the day and let students know what will be happening. An agenda can be used to model making a list of things to be accomplished. Teachers can go back to the agenda with the

Figure 5–3. A posted daily schedule helps students follow the sequence of their "very busy day."

students and check off what has been done, continually evaluating how the class is using its time and soliciting student input by asking questions like "Will we have time to get to author's chair this morning?" Students can suggest how to fit an event into the schedule or when to reschedule.

When teachers refer to the time blocks in the daily routine ("It's writer's workshop time now; get your writing folders"), students are cued as to what is expected of them and can plan ahead and participate in a positive way. This is helpful to young children who are still learning how to function in a group setting and to older children who are learning how to organize their time and work.

Provide Sufficient Blocks of Time

Students must be given time blocks that are long enough to let them become involved in their work. In order to get absorbed in a piece of writing, artwork, or a science or math exploration, students need enough time to get over initial starts and stops. Reaching this level of focus is one of the joys of learning and students should not be rushed in order to fit more activities into the day. Too many activities and the resultant transitions make the classroom day a harried exercise where a lot is touched upon but not much is really covered. As they get to know their students and classroom routines smooth out, teachers can predict how much time students will need to produce satisfying work. Work periods begin with a flurry as students get materials, get situated, and settle in. If work periods are too short, many students never get beyond the settling-in period to get anything accomplished. Although a classroom community will use time more efficiently as they learn the routines, both children and adults will always need time to focus on the matter at hand and delve into it in a meaningful way.

The teacher must be aware of individual differences, which extend to students' work style and pace. Some students will need extra time to get started on their work. Knowing this, teachers may allow a little extra time or engage students in a conversation about their work to help them warm up and take off. For example, a child having trouble writing during writer's workshop may need just a quick conversation to help clarify the ideas she is thinking of writing about. Students who have a hard time wrapping up their work may need support in the form of more personally directed announcements about "finishing-up time," help thinking through what to do next, or the teacher's indulgence about being the last one finished.

Provide Clear Procedures and Shared Routines

Clear procedures and shared routines foster a sense of group identity because they provide a common way of approaching the demands of daily life. The ways a class starts the day; begins and ends units of study; deals with issues that come up; celebrates special events; and transitions through the day, week, and year all give a class a certain personality and common frame of reference.

At the beginning of the day, third-grade students in Wendy Smithers' class perform routines that mesh with academic goals. They go to tables of four and work together on "incredible equations" whose answers must equal the date. They also locate and record daily information on a world weather chart (learning to read maps and graphs) or a world travel airfare chart (for example, by applying the value of today's yen in U.S. dollars to airfares). The "big cheese" of the week locates the day, date, and month and the whole class figures out multiplication equations for the number of days they have been in school (learning the commutative property and multiplication facts, as well as highlighting prime numbers).

Students must be explicitly taught clear procedures in order to function independently within the daily routine. Whenever children move from one activity to the next, whether from inside to outside or from sitting down to standing up, there is the potential for chaos and confusion. Everything seems to go along smoothly until it is time to move from point A to point B. That is often when arguments and fights break out, complaints are voiced, someone is lagging, and someone is unprepared. Such confusion is usually due to a lack of clarity about the teacher's expectations for the students' behavior during the transition. Along with demonstrating how a transition can go smoothly, teachers can remind students a few minutes before a change will take place. When students and teachers construct expectations for functioning together and refer back to them at class meetings, students can take responsibility for how the class transitions.

All disciplines are marked by attention to the tools or instruments needed to get the work done: A painter carefully cleans her brushes; a musician takes great care in storing his instrument. Care for the physical environment of the classroom doesn't just happen. Carefully introducing materials and using a "guided discovery" approach (Charney 1992) to new materials contributes to students' sense of responsibility. Writer's workshop, note-taking on field trips, choosing a book, circling up in P.E., doing homework—the range of activities we ask students to undertake during the school year continues to grow. Multiple languages, learning styles, and individual differences all contribute to the need to introduce new activities carefully. When teachers demonstrate each step, show what materials to use and how to use them, and make expectations for the end product clear, students can become self-reliant. This is especially true of small-group activities. Ann Park helps her students get organized by providing folders for each curriculum area and showing how to use them. Sally Kaneko's class has "binder business" at the end of the day to organize students' packing up.

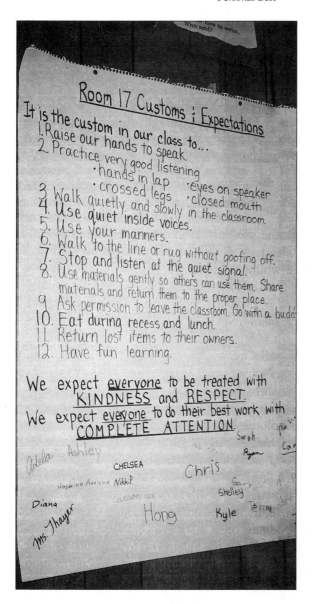

Figure 5–4. Clear expectations for behavior are communicated through a "customs and expectations" chart, brainstormed and signed by all students in a third-grade classroom.

Allow Time for Interaction and Collaboration

Time for interaction and collaboration among students is key to the daily routine. Using small groups in the classroom maximizes the opportunity for students to carry out work independently, a critical aspect of the learning process. Interacting in small groups allows students to refine their own thinking by checking their ideas against the ideas of their peers. Vygotsky viewed language as central to learning.

> Language, the primary cultural tool used by humans to mediate their activities, is instrumental in restructuring the mind and in forming higher-order, self-regulated thought processes. (Berk and Winsler 1995)

Children working in small groups are noisy. They make comments, ask questions, tease, joke, and converse on topics that may be considered "off-task." This is all part of young minds at work, trying to make connections between events,

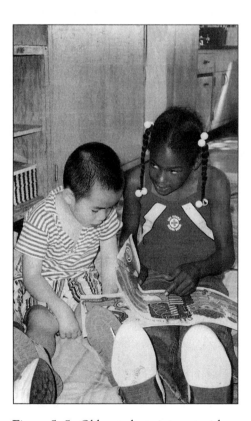

Figure 5–5. Older students interact with younger students through buddy reading, a time to read aloud and share favorite books.

checking out their viewpoints with others, and negotiating solutions. Children are keenly observant of one another's work and watch and compare expectantly. They often can explain a concept to a peer more effectively than an adult can. When given opportunities to work together, children learn how to accept the ideas of others and build on them. When they are helped to learn how to work together harmoniously, they learn lifelong teamwork skills.

Daily opportunities to work in small groups are an important feature of learner-centered classrooms. Small-group work fosters students' independence and interdependence. Some teachers require that students ask peers to answer questions before coming to the teacher. Janet Gore uses the rhyme "one, two, three, then me" to remind children to ask three peers before asking her. Small-group work can allow students to work in more depth on an activity. The group effort pushes students and keeps them engaged as they learn from their peers. On a practical level, working in small groups means that only four to six children use materials at the same time, so a class set of materials is not needed to do an activity. On a management level, all students get a turn to talk and use the materials so there is less waiting, boredom, and disengagement. Probably the most important benefit from the teacher's point of view is that using small groups lets them tailor instruction to individuals and begin to meet the wide range of skills, interests, and styles of the children in the classroom.

Provide Time to Process and Reflect

Reflecting on work accomplished and shared experiences brings closure to a busy day. A classroom workshop or project can be wrapped up in an end-of-day "debriefing" that gives students the opportunity to talk about how their work went, what they learned, what they might do next time, etc., and gives small groups a chance to hear from one another. One way to debrief is to call a class meeting and ask everyone in the circle to talk a little about their work. If students have been working in small groups, each group can report on what they did and possibly show their products. If another group will be rotating to that activity, a teacher might ask, "Is there anything you would like to tell the next group that does this activity?" This builds a connection between students and identifies students as resources.

We have seen small-group work fall apart because there was no accountability for the end product or the quality of time spent. Debriefing lets students know that their efforts are valued, that both the teacher and the other class members are interested in their work. Sometimes in a busy day, teachers and students can feel that they are just running from one thing to the next to fit it all in. Debriefing can be a way to build reflection and appreciation into the day and can give teachers valuable information about the effectiveness of the learning experiences they planned.

Students need time to process and reflect on what they have learned and how they have learned it. This consolidates their learning and helps both students and teacher shape the learning process. All students, regardless of their performance level, need to be engaged in reflection and communicating their thinking. In Japanese schools, *hansei*, self-evaluation and reflection, accompanies learning activities across the curriculum. Hansei can include both individual and group reflection on what worked well and what needed improvement (Lewis 1995).

Reflection takes many forms in learner-centered classrooms, including logs, journals, exit slips, and group discussions of the learning process. The form of reflection used needs to help both the students and the teacher extend their knowledge and plan new learning opportunities. A simple literature log in which a student writes her thoughts about what she has just read is a powerful tool for the student to construct meaning. Math reflections show concretely how a student solved a problem and give the teacher information that lets her target instruction.

Showcase Best Work Through Mastery Events

"Mastery events" that showcase students' best work can bring closure to focused study and demonstrate students' new knowledge and competence to an outside audience. A mastery event could be a presentation of students' projects or an exhibit that parents and other classes are invited to attend. It could be a party where students prepare a special snack. Mastery events become part of many classrooms' traditions, and students in other grades watch those events with anticipation or a sense of nostalgia for the past.

Laura Burges ends each year with a literary tea party. Parents drink tea and eat cookies as students recite poetry they have memorized as a whole group. Each child then reads a short piece of their own fiction or nonfiction. Carole Seligman celebrates with her third graders when each child has published a book, and again when everyone in the class has published. When the class has published one hundred books, students invite the second graders in to listen to their stories and decorate the room with "about the authors" posters.

On the hundredth day of the school year, students in Janet Gore's community eat one hundred things, build with one hundred manipulatives, write a story with one hundred words, and commemorate the hundredth day at the end of the day. Children look forward to the hundredth day celebration from the first day of school, keeping track of the number of days with straws divided into tens and ones during opening time each morning.

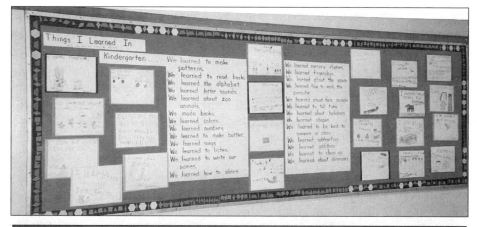

Figure 5–6. Students reflect on their learning through drawing and writing.

Sara Nielsen's fourth-grade's study of Native Americans culminated in removing desks and transforming the classroom into a Native American museum that showcased student-made baskets, pottery, and models of shelters. Students acted as docents and ticket takers and performed other museum functions as parents and other classes were given tours. First-grade teacher Pamela Meyers invites parents and siblings to become paleontologists for the night as her students lead them through hands-on activities to culminate their study of dinosaurs. At the all-school level, West Portal School students host an academic fair and open house. Some classrooms hold potlucks and others have booths. Demonstrations are set up in the auditorium, and each classroom makes its best work available to show parents and to talk about.

Mastery events let students showcase their personal best efforts and model high standards for academic work for each other. Teachers can save student work from these events to use as examples for next year's class, making "personal best" explicit from the first days of school.

6

Engagement

Children have inquiring minds. By the time most children in the United States are five years old, they have acquired a vocabulary of roughly five thousand words, internalized a thousand rules of grammar, and acquired boundless information about the people, places, and things in their world. Yet elementary schooling has developed to the point where teachers feel that they do not have the time, space, or support needed to allow children to wonder, choose their own topics, explore, and conduct research.

Inquiry is what all children do best. Research into how the brain develops and how human beings acquire knowledge leads us to conclude that powerful learning occurs when students can become immersed in a topic, put their hands on the real thing, search out patterns, and put information into the big picture. An active, engaging classroom allows students at a range of developmental levels to make use of multiple intelligences to learn about a subject. It embeds the "hard" information we want our students to learn in larger and more meaningful contexts while teaching problem-solving, investigative, and "how-to" skills that last a lifetime.

Through research and community projects, students become highly engaged as they are surrounded by stories, real people, real places, and primary sources from which to gather information. As teachers observe students' preconceptions, they learn about the theories that students have constructed to explain the world and can then help students revise their thinking. As students choose their own topics of research, students feel motivated and the whole class gains new knowledge. Using a special project to culminate a learning activity gives students a sense of pride and accomplishment, demonstrates what they learned and how they learned it to the community. Planning, carrying out, and reviewing projects gives teachers and students the opportunity for instruction, guided research, and first hand discovery.

Activate Prior Knowledge

All knowledge is influenced by prior knowledge. As learners, we are not blank slates. Even infants use prior experience, albeit extremely recent, to respond to new input. A student's prior experiences form her expectations and assumptions about how the world works. And because students bring their experiences as members of a cultural group to school, family and cultural values help determine what students will value and respond to in the classroom.

When we launch a unit of study, we are speaking to a classroom full of students with their own assumptions and worldviews. New input is filtered through those assumptions and changed as learners make associations to what they already know. It is critical to access and link to prior knowledge at the onset of a project. For example, when students begin to study Native Americans, they may have stereotypes from the popular culture. By asking students to draw how they think Native peoples once lived, the teacher can evoke students' misconceptions. By asking students what they have heard about a subject, teachers can address and challenge misconceptions and give students a chance to reevaluate their assumptions.

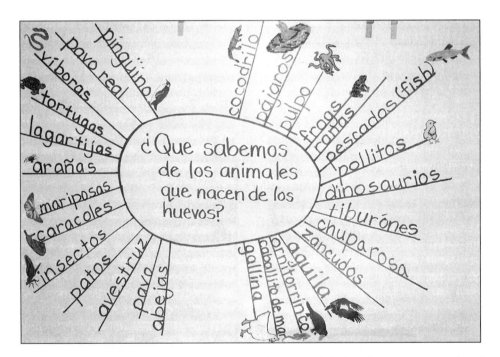

Figure 6–1. Prior knowledge is discussed and organized before beginning a study of "animals that come from eggs."

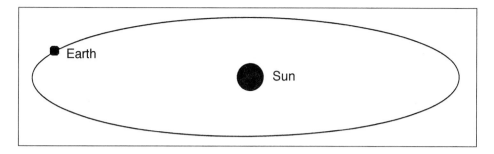

Figure 6–2. A perspective drawing of the earth's orbit can create a misconception that the changing distance from the sun, rather than the tilt of the earth's axis, causes the seasons.

In *A Private Universe: Misconceptions That Block Learning*, a film by Matthew Schneps, students graduating from Harvard are asked to explain what causes the seasons (1989). Graduate after graduate, in cap and gown, explains that the seasons are the result of the earth's elliptical movement around the sun rather than its rotation on an axis. The film goes on to illustrate that the students have probably carried this assumption with them unchallenged through their entire school life, based on their early experience with science textbooks in which two-dimensional perspective drawings of the earth's orbital movement represent the orbit as a highly exaggerated ellipse.

Accessing prior knowledge is a simple step. Asking students what they already know can inform our teaching in critical ways while showing students that we respect what they bring with them into the classroom. It also lays the groundwork for significant learning to take place.

Activating students' prior knowledge also calls forth a wealth of lived experience, giving richness to their reading and writing experiences. Each person brings their own prior knowledge and unique perspective to the reading of a text.

Engage Students in Authentic Experience and Experimentation

Children's interests and need to know motivate learning and their lived daily experiences and natural curiosity give teachers open avenues for making classroom work meaningful. Swiss psychologist Jean Piaget wrote that "authentic work" is a basic characteristic of active education:

> When the active school requires that the student's effort should come from the student himself instead of being imposed, and that his intelligence should undertake authentic work instead of accepting predigested knowledge from the outside, it is therefore simply asking that the laws of all intelligence should be respected. (1969, 159)

Brain research supports Piaget's notion: A child is born with billions of neurons, some already "hardwired" by genetic material into circuits that control breathing, heartbeat, body temperature, or reflexes. But millions more neurons are waiting to be programmed through the child's interactions with the environment. As the child plays, neurons are stimulated and connected to one another. In an enriched environment the brain builds more neural networks, thus increasing its weight and density (Diamond and Hopson 1998).

What children attend to in the environment and the ways in which they respond to stimuli determine the physical structure of their brains—how many networks they have and how elaborate or sophisticated they are. No matter how well planned, interesting, stimulating, colorful, or relevant a lesson, if the teacher does all the interacting with the material, it is the teacher's brain—not the student's—that will grow. An enriched environment gives students' brains many opportunities for active engagement.

The closer a learning experience is to the "real thing," the more senses it evokes and the more sensory input the brain receives. For example, if the class is studying flowers, you would visit a garden or wildflower patch or plant some flowers, watch them grow, and compare and contrast them. Only after these concrete experiences would you use models, videos, and books to teach the students more.

Educational psychologists and brain researchers have concluded that learning occurs best when the experience is authentic and the learner is actively engaged in the process. We learn and retain 80 percent of what we experience directly and 10 to 20 percent of what we see and hear.

Francisco Hernandez gives coffee filters to his fourth-/fifth-grade bilingual students as they take a field trip to the zoo. They gather seeds, feathers, stones, and leaves—whatever treasures they find. They watch a dandelion seed float through the air like a parachute. Hernandez picks up on their interest, asking, "How does it travel like that?" Back in the classroom, students pair up and try to build models that will float through the air.

Observing, testing, retesting, analyzing, hypothesizing, and revising theories based on new information is as much the work of a child as it is the work of a scientist. Children wonder What makes this work? Does it always do this? What if I change it somehow? How do I make it do it again? Engaging students in meaningful experiences draws them into the curriculum, connecting to their own interests and feeding their natural curiosity.

Carole Edelsky (1986) and others have pointed out the importance of authenticity in literacy events. Writing for the real world gives meaning to student experience. When Betty Doerr asked her fifth-grade students if they had any input for a community meeting about drug dealers around their playground, hands shot

I was holding a millepede. The millepede was tickling my hand. The millepede almost went on my arm.

Figure 6–3. The excitement of authentic experience is conveyed by a student's caption on a photo of himself holding a millipede.

up. The result was thirty letters about the students' experiences, which moved the community to take action.

There are many moments that call for a genuine response from students. In a learning community we are constantly on the lookout for such moments. Elzaida Alcaide's writer's workshop for her fourth- and fifth-grade Tagalog-English bilingual students has produced gold, silver, and bronze award–winning essays in the citywide Language Academy Olympics on "Why I Value My Two Languages."

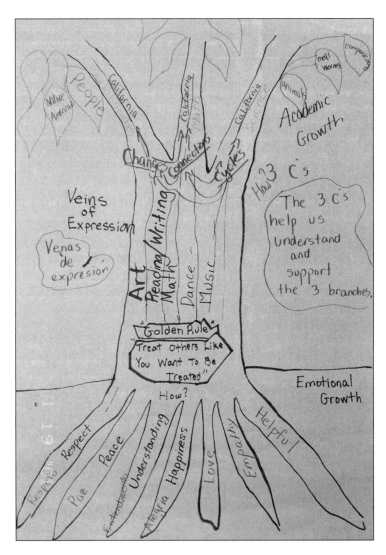

Figure 6–4. A large poster of the "Elder Tree" in a fifth-grade classroom uses the imagery of roots, trunk, and branches to guide their integrated unit.

On entering Robert Marosi's classroom, you are immediately drawn to an illustration on the wall, titled "The Elders Are Watching," that depicts Marosi's approach to integrating social development and the academic curriculum.

The roots of Marosi's "elder tree" represent areas of social and emotional growth—respect, peace, understanding, happiness, love, empathy, and helpfulness. Marosi explains: "I try to give students the idea that we all have our roots, our emotional growth—which include things such as conflict management." The roots support the tree trunk, which represents "veins of expression"—art, reading, writing, math, dance, music. These veins feed into three branches of academic growth and maturity. The three themes of these branches—cycles, changes, and connections—support and broaden understanding of the subject. Marosi integrates the curriculum through themes. He comments,

> When we're studying California, we study through these different themes. Cycles, for example, are more conducive to science, so I tend to focus on cycles when I'm teaching science. Connections are the main focus when I teach math, and changes when we learn about first peoples—California history from the native peoples to the missions. The investigation of the first peoples relates to their connection with nature—for example, they did a study on acorns, with mortar, pestle, seeds, and getting out the tannins. Integration of subjects is built in.

Ask Probing Questions

Learners can reach a comfort zone when their view of the world is working nicely for them. Prompting students with new input that does not fit with their previously held assumptions challenges them to reach for new understandings. Development occurs when learners rethink previously held assumptions (Fosnot 1991).

Loris Malaguzzi, director of early childhood programs in Reggio Emilia, Italy, that have received worldwide recognition, believes that "touching, feeling, and smelling are not the same as asking, experimenting, and speculating" (1993). The teacher's role is to push students to rethink by asking probing questions, evoking alternative explanations ("what-if'") and challenging students to articulate their ideas. Questioning is one of the oldest, simplest, and most powerful teaching strategies. Hogan and Pressley (1997, 90) describe what kinds of statements prompt student thinking:

A teacher statement that prompts student thinking...
- Frames a problem or articulates a goal. ("It sounds to me like you're trying to figure out why the force indicator had a higher reading the second time.")

- Encourages attention to conflicts and differences of opinion. ("Jenny, Tom thinks the answer is *humid* and you think it's *arid*. I want you to keep talking to each other and figure it out.")
- Refocuses the discussion. ("So far we've agreed on one thing—let's consider data from the second experiment.")
- Invites interaction of ideas. ("What's James asking? Who can expand on that?")
- Prompts refinement of language. ("When you say *it* went up, what exactly are you referring to? What do you mean when you say *air pressure?*")
- Turns a question back to its owner. ("I don't know, what do you think?")
- Communicates standards for explanations. ("I need to hear the evidence that backs up your claim.")
- Asks for elaboration. ("So talk to us about the angles you mentioned.")
- Asks for clarification. ("You need to tell me what you mean when you say *whatever the liquid consists of*.")
- Restates or summarizes student statements. ("So you're saying that with a large surface area and the same weight, the disk would move farther?")

Robert Marosi stands with his fourth-grade Spanish-English bilingual students in their garden in San Francisco's Mission District. He holds up a seed pod:

ROBERT: How come you can't see flowers anymore on this fava bean?
DAVID: A little hummingbird came.
ROBERT: A little hummingbird came and what?
DAVID: Sucked the nectar—and got the male part and the female part.
ROBERT: What did he get?
DAVID: The powder.
ROBERT: What is it called?
DAVID: Pollen.
ROBERT: So then what happened? (waits) So now the female has this little sticky part, right? and then the pollen hit the sticky part, and then what happened to it? Where does the pollen go? It's already in the female part. . . (waits) Now, this is the part of the story we're at. Does everyone understand—the female part now has the pollen on it. What is the female going to do?
MANUEL: The female part makes seeds.
ROBERT: Did anyone hear him? Wait a second. The female part makes *seeds?*
STUDENTS: Yes.
ROBERT: Does that make sense?
SOME STUDENTS: Yes.
DAVID AND ALEX: It doesn't make seeds, it makes eggs.

ROBERT TO STUDENTS WHO SAID "YES": It makes sense?

OTHER STUDENTS: It doesn't make seeds, it makes eggs.

ROBERT: Plants have male and female parts, right? Do flowers have eggs?

STUDENTS: Yes.

ROBERT: How many people think flowers have eggs? Good. So now you know: The plant has a female part—the female part has a tube—the pollen goes down the tube and the dust hits the eggs and what does it do to the eggs?

GABRIELA: Turns them into. . .

ROBERT: Turns them into what?

STUDENTS: SEEDS.

ROBERT: So this is what has happened here (holding up fava bean). So what was here (touching fava plant) before?

STUDENTS: FLOWERS!

ROBERT: Exactly. There were flowers here before. You can tell. Right here at the end of it you can see where the flower was, and you can see one of the favas still has a flower on it and that means it has not been. . .

STUDENTS: POLLINATED!

Here we see young minds at work as a teacher asks his students what they know and pushes them to explain, clarify, and draw conclusions. Some students then weed, water, and harvest. Others closely examine flowers and make anatomical sketches in their notebooks. One boy exclaims, "Robert, Robert, look at this!" as he sees the reproductive process at work within his flower.

7

Support to Independence

We cannot demand their personal best from students if we don't have a precise notion of what their best work might look like. Teachers want to help children reach high standards by knowing who they are, where they are academically, and where they need to go next. Learner-centered teachers use a variety of ways to get to know and then reach students in order to meet their real needs in a supportive way. These are the "how's" of teaching, the pedagogy.

Identify Students' Learning Zones

Although individuals are thought to construct their own knowledge internally (Piaget and Inhelder 1971), they do not engage in this process alone. Vygotsky posited that learners advance by interacting with others and construct ideas as a result of interaction and negotiation:

> Learning awakens a variety of internal developmental processes that are able to operate only when the child is interacting with people from his environment and in cooperation with his peers. Once these processes are internalized, they become part of the child's independent developmental achievement. (1978, 89)

Dewey described the provision of these experiences as the main role of the teacher (Cuffaro 1994). As children try out new ideas, concepts, and procedures, the teacher provides the support or assistance— the "scaffolding"—necessary for new learning. A classroom climate that is conducive to social interaction, cooperative grouping, partner work, active learning, probing questions, modeling, direct instruction, and guided practice provides such scaffolding. This concept of "support to independence" is based on Vygotsky's work on the role of social interaction in learning and is key to what goes on in successful communities of learners (see Figure 7–1, p. 92). Support to independence is the continual scaffolding that each student needs to reach beyond her current performance level. The goal is for students to be able to function independently and to successfully carry out increasingly difficult tasks.

When students get the scaffolding they need for learning to take place, they increasingly internalize what they have experienced and make it their own. Vygotsky (1986) describes this process of internalization as "an operation that initially represents an external activity that is reconstructed and begins to occur internally." This is not internalization in the behavioral sense of concepts being spoon-fed to students. The Goodmans (1990) believe that children learn concepts through the push and pull of personal invention and social convention. Some developmentalists have used the term "guided reinvention" to describe the process by which students internalize information through active involvement.

Identifying students' learning zones plays a critical role in assessing their learner characteristics. Learner characteristics include age-related issues, qualities unique to the individual, students' cultural contexts (Bredekamp and Copple 1997), and students' learning zones. Activities within a student's "zone of actual development" are ones he can carry out independently, without teacher guidance. Students carrying out independent activities feel a sense of competence and confidence. In a classroom, students can carry out activities in the zone of actual development alone or working in centers or at stations.

On the other end of the spectrum are activities in the "frustration zone"—the things a particular student cannot yet do either alone or with assistance. Students who are assigned to do independent or small-group activities in their frustration zone may shut down, avoid the task, or find someone else to do the work. Teachers sometimes mistakenly assign homework that is in the frustration zone, hoping to cover material they are required to teach. Even with the parent stepping in to do the actual work, little real learning takes place. Without support a student is left frustrated and feeling incompetent. However, new information that would be in the frustration zone can be introduced at the awareness or exposure level in a heavily supported whole-group situation where no demand for performance is placed on a child.

Between the actual development zone and the frustration zone lies the "learning zone," or the "zone of proximal development" (ZPD). This is the area of tasks that children can perform with assistance but not alone. It is a prime area for teaching, particularly in an individual or guided small-group setting where there is opportunity for intense teacher support.

Just as students are constantly developing, teachers are constantly assessing, planning, and adapting, using learner characteristics to shape the learning process.

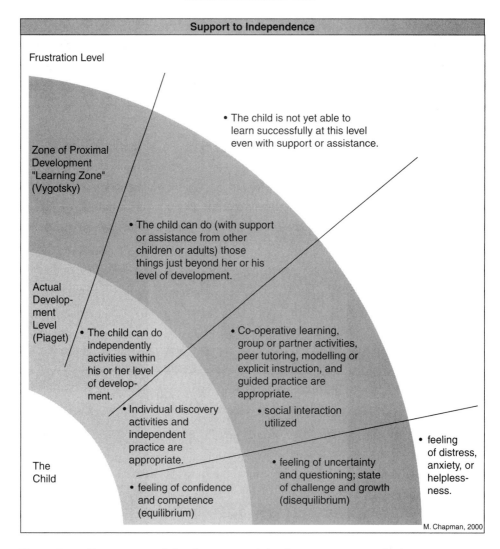

Figure 7–1. Between actual development and the frustration zone is the learning zone, a prime area for teaching and support.

It remains necessary to determine the lowest threshold at which instruction in, say, arithmetic may begin, since a certain minimal ripeness of functions is required. But we must consider the upper threshold as well; instruction must be pointed toward the future, not the past. (Vygotsky 1986, 188–189)

In a community of learners, teachers do not view students statically ("He reads on a first-grade level") but as being in motion in an upward spiral ("He needs work on reading words in context and books on his instructional level to become a more fluent reader"). Assessment is focused on gathering ideas for intervention and discovering ways to facilitate the student's learning, knowing that the student can and will learn once offered the time and means to do so.

How do teachers maintain dynamic relationships so they can reach each student within their zone of proximal development across several subject areas? Teachers use an array of strategies to assess and document growth. First-grade teacher Kathy Rosebrock makes use of the concept "uses but confuses" from *Words Their Way* (Bear et al. 2000) to determine which skills students have and which they use but confuse. These budding skills are in the zone of proximal development— the learning zone—where the teacher's intervention will have the most impact. Rosebrock explains how looking at what a student "uses but confuses" helps her analyze students' work and know when and how to intervene:

> Gathering and saving student work is an excellent way to observe progress over time. Regular analysis of student work samples can give a clear picture of what the student can do at any given time and what growth the student has made over time. This analysis can be organized around three main questions that uncover information for planning instruction for the whole class and for individual students:
>
> - *What can the child already do correctly?* Work samples that show what the student can do correctly on her own at this time indicate what we can expect her to do correctly in the future. The student is now working on making these tasks automatic.
> - *What does the student use but confuse?* Work samples show which skills the student knows about and is trying to use but has not yet mastered. For example, a student who is beginning to use periods at the end of sentences but isn't sure what a sentence is might put a period at the end of each line instead of each sentence. This is a powerful clue for teachers that this is the challenge the student has chosen to work on. A little targeted time spent with this student could help him make this task something he can do correctly.
> - *What is absent?* What might be next on the continuum of development but is not yet evident in the student's work? Asking this question gives information about what to introduce to the class or to individual students—which topics to demonstrate to the whole group or to plan small-group lessons around. Students need to be introduced to the vocabulary and to get a beginning understanding of new skills and strategies before they can try them out on their own.

These three questions are especially helpful when used to assess student writing. By keeping samples of student writing over time, it is possible to observe skills or concepts that students found confusing while moving up to mastery level. Writing samples from Tom, a first-grade student, taken in September, November, and April and the related teacher notes on his progress give a clear picture of Tom's growth over time:

- September. Tom's writing—the pictures he drew and the story he dictated about a dog and a cat—shows that he has an idea of story narrative. He shows an understanding of print by labeling the picture with a familiar word ("DOG"). Tom knows about left-to-right progression. There is some confusion in the area of letter formation and size. In labeling both pictures with the same word, Tom shows that he isn't sure about matching words with pictures, nor is he sure of what the letters "DOG" represent, since he uses the label "DOG" for both the dog and the cat. Tom relies on memorized or copied words and uses no phonics or other strategies to spell words. There is not yet evidence of his thoughts in print. Lowercase letters are not used.

  This sample sheds light on what might be the next steps for Tom's writing development. The aspects of writing that he is using but confusing are challenges that he has chosen to work on. With a little help, these skills can be perfected. The elements of writing that are not yet in place would be good topics to introduce in a whole-group setting and through teacher demonstrations. Lessons might be planned to introduce and practice these new skills.

- November. There is a big change in Tom's work. He can now get print on paper and has a sense of using story language to relate his story to others. Left-to-right progression is clear. Letter size and letter case are still in the "uses but confuses" area, as is Tom's use of phonics to spell words on his own. Tom has shown a huge jump in his writing ability since September. Still absent are the use of punctuation other than periods and the use of capital letters. These would be good topics to introduce to Tom at this time.

- April. Tom can now put his thoughts and stories on paper quite efficiently. He has many words spelled correctly and his handwriting is very legible. He shows evidence of the use of periods and capital letters, though they are not always used in the right place. There is some confusion in the letters "b," "d," and "p." These skills have moved up from being absent in the November sample and are now in the "uses but confuses" area, making them perfect topics for individual targeted work with Tom. There is evidence of dialogue in the writing, but no use of quotation marks. The use of "ed" for past tense is also absent. Tom would benefit from demonstrations or mini-lessons on these topics.

Learner-centered teachers make assessment an ongoing practice that is embedded in their daily and weekly routines. To develop an assessment system that works, teachers may want to do the following:

- Choose a format that works for you (clipboard, binder, etc.).
- Have regular times when the assessment can be done (daily during independent reading, three times a week, etc.).

Student Tom

Grade 1st

1. What student does correctly.... Tells story through pictures. Labels picture (dog) Writes with left to right progression Writes words from memory

2. What student uses but confuses.... Meaning of letters d·o·g. Letter size and formation

3. What is absent.... Phonetic / temporary spelling is absent. Not yet writing complete thoughts on paper. Use of lowercase letters is absent

Figure 7-2. In September, Tom copied the date from the board and drew a picture to represent a story about his dog and a neighborhood cat. He verbally told the story and labeled the cat and the dog with letters "d-o-g."

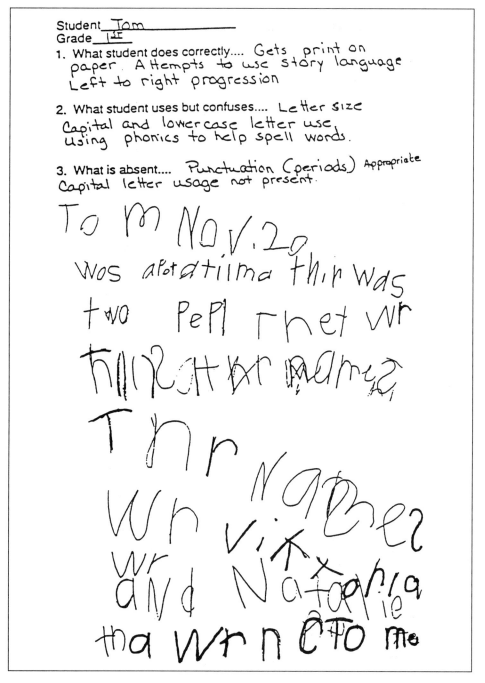

Student ___Tom_____

Grade ___I__

1. What student does correctly.... Gets print on paper. Attempts to use story language Left to right progression

2. What student uses but confuses.... Letter size Capital and lowercase letter use, using phonics to help spell words.

3. What is absent.... Punctuation (periods) Appropriate Capital letter usage not present.

To M NOV. 20

Wos aPotatiilma thir was
two PePl rhet wr
hilirht r mamr,
Thr nam r
Wr Viktoria
and Natalia
tha wrn cto me

Figure 7–3. In November, Tom wrote: "Once upon a time there were two people. They were friends and their names were Viktoria and Natalie. They were nice to me."

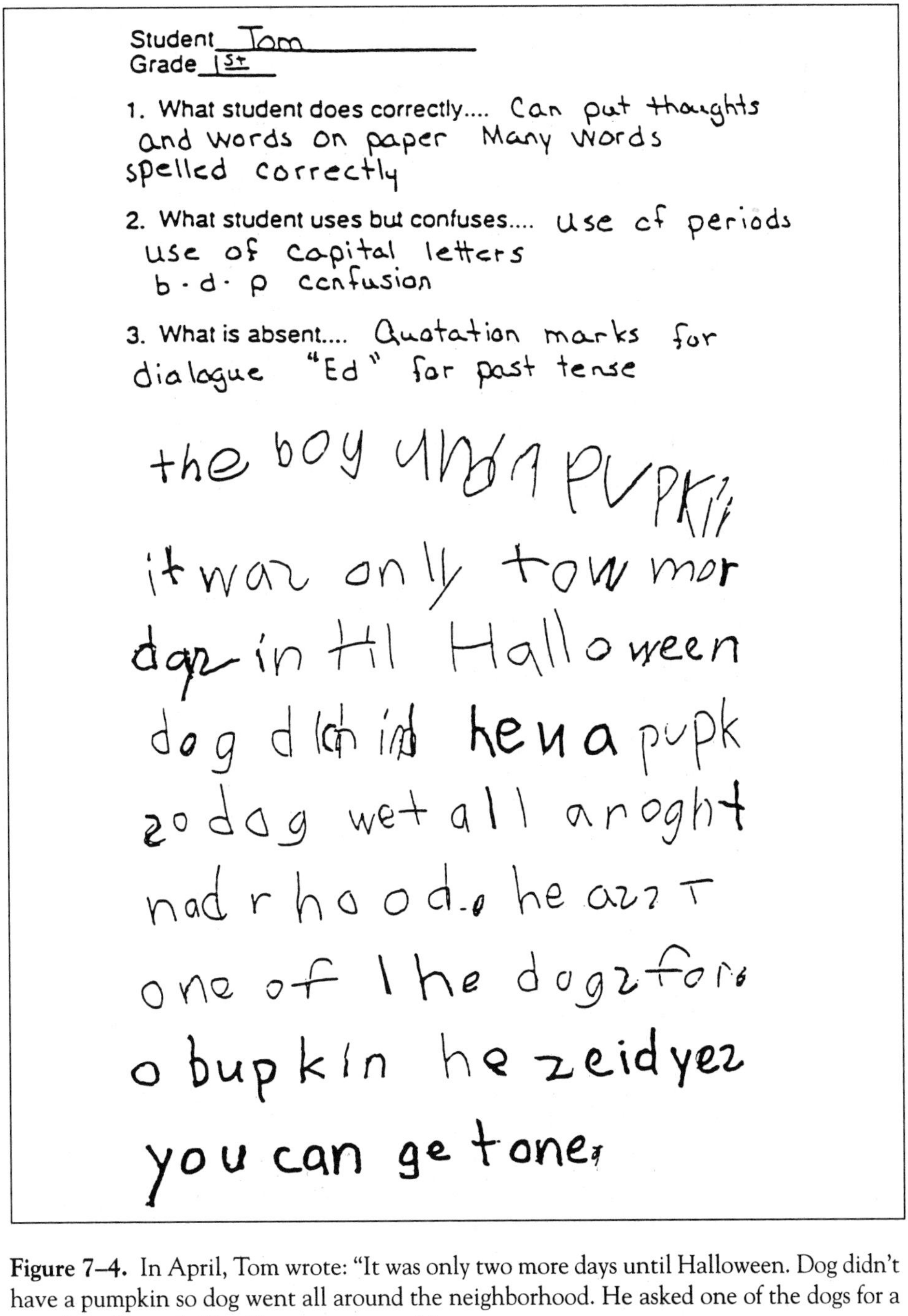

Student **Tom**
Grade **1st**

1. What student does correctly.... Can put thoughts and words on paper Many words spelled correctly

2. What student uses but confuses.... use of periods use of capital letters b·d· p confusion

3. What is absent.... Quotation marks for dialogue "Ed" for past tense

the boy und a PUPKI

it war only tow mor

dgp in til Halloween

dog d ldh id hen a pupk

zo dog wet all an oght

nad r ho od. he azz T

one of l he dogz for

o bupkin he zeidyez

you can ge tone;

Figure 7–4. In April, Tom wrote: "It was only two more days until Halloween. Dog didn't have a pumpkin so dog went all around the neighborhood. He asked one of the dogs for a pumpkin. He said, 'Yes. You can get one.' "

- Have a schedule or routine that ensures that each child is being assessed regularly.
- Have clear objectives for your assessment (one to three points are manageable).
- Have a clear system for follow-up activities based on what you have assessed (whole-class mini-lesson, guided reading group, individual or paired guidance and support).
- Think through how this information will be recorded for report cards or parent conferences.

While assessment must be practical and fit easily into the daily routine, the kind of assessment Vygotsky had in mind represents an attitude, a daily habit of kid-watching. In a caring, supportive atmosphere, teacher assessment and follow-up allow students to grasp new material and move to higher levels of understanding. This is the heart of teaching, where teacher and learner meet to propel the student toward independence.

Maximize Time in the Learning Zone

For at least two reasons, whole-class instruction—the most common activity setting in American and Canadian classrooms—works poorly to achieve the negotiation of shared meaning necessary to guide children through successive ZPDs. First, the teacher cannot adequately attend to the instructional needs of individual children. Second, to maintain order and a smooth flow of classroom events, whole-class teaching requires constant asymmetry of power between teachers and children. . . . When children are granted no more than a reactive voice in classroom dialogues, they have little opportunity to experiment with strategies under the watchful eye of an adult expert and to indicate (through verbal or behavioral cues) the kind of assistance they need to achieve meaningful understanding. (Berk and Winsler 1995, 116)

According to Berk and Winsler, in whole-class settings an unexpected answer frequently prompts the teacher to move on to another student, until the anticipated answer is given. In a major study of thirty-eight schools in diverse communities and regions, Goodlad found that "on the average, only 7 of 150 minutes of the school day involved a teacher responding to a student's work" (Tharp and Gallimore 1988). When whole-class instruction, quizzes, and worksheets are the primary means of instruction, it is difficult to provide students with support to independence.

When assessment reveals a problem or concept that involves a majority of the class, whole-group instruction may be in order, but it can be whole-group instruction of another sort. Mary Tudor noted that most of the fourth-grade students in her multilingual classroom did not grasp the concept of "compare and contrast." Tudor used the book *Babe the Gallant Pig*, by Dick King-Smith. She first showed the video and the whole class mapped the story. The map provided much of the vocabulary the children would encounter in reading the story and gave them a basis for comparing and contrasting. The whole class worked on the first three chapters of the book, writing a summary and modeling a chart to compare and contrast the book and video for each chapter. The rest of the book was divided among small groups, who prepared their chapter to share with the class, giving a summary and comparing and contrasting the book and video for their chapter. All the students were both engaged and successful. By the end of the process, the class had a clear grasp of the concept "compare and contrast."

Feedback is critical to providing support to independence. A community where students truly learn requires frequent opportunities for teacher and peer feedback and response, including coaching and guidance at the instructional level. The term "guided instruction" or "assisted instruction" has been used to describe the scaffolding that teachers provide to students in the learning zone. Guided instruction occurs in the zone of proximal development. The teacher meets with students individually or in groups that have a like need. Instruction is focused, materials offer an optimal level of challenge, and the teacher uses support strategies to help the children stretch to a new level. The teacher recognizes each student's learner characteristics and creates a climate of mutual respect where the voice of each student is valued.

Assessment is an integral part of guided instruction. Groups for guided instruction change frequently, depending on the needs of the individuals. As a student or small group grasps a new concept or strategy, the teacher withdraws to allow them to try out their newfound knowledge, fumble, and correct themselves. The teacher intervenes only when a student can't move forward. Berk and Winsler (1995) point out that "as soon as a common goal is established, a combination of active withdrawal by the adult in response to active takeover by the child is crucial for the development of self-regulation." They go on to point out that when adults give immediate answers to momentary problems or continually give explicit commands, students' learning and self-regulation are diminished. Question-and-answer formats or round-robin reading are not good uses of guided instruction, as they build reliance on the teacher to give the right answer or the missing word.

Independent reading and writing and independent small-group work can be used when the learning process calls for students to process ideas or practice new skills and strategies in their zone of actual development. Having some students work independently frees the teacher up to focus on individuals or small groups of students who need instruction in the learning zone. Extended time for students to read independently, then respond in writing in a spiral notebook, lets students work in their zone of actual development, as does giving students extended time to work independently in a writers' workshop. Teachers can design centers or stations for small-group work where students can practice and extend new strategies and skills on their own independent level.

Glendi Henion-Ul sees center time as "an important time for observing behavior and noting language development, social skills, and areas which may need to be addressed at a more structured time. Afterwards I debrief with the children. Children share what they've learned and experienced during centers to develop oral language skills."

The teacher can have groups rotate among literacy centers that the teacher has designed to give them practice in various aspects of the literacy program, such as word work, literature extension and response activities, and use of the computer. Henion-Ul's literacy centers include:

alphabet center
writing center (children can use a variety of writing materials to create their own stories, books, etc.)
poetry center
tracing center
book area
listening center

Students also have the opportunity to work with:

sentence strips
overhead projector
dry-erase boards
chalkboards
handwriting worksheets
computers
"reading the room" (children use pointers and involve themselves in environmental print)
flannel board stories
beads, puzzles, magnetic letters, etc. to build fine motor skills

Some teachers prefer to use "menus" of activities in a particular academic area, instead of centers or stations, to give students time to work independently while the teacher intervenes with individuals or in small groups. Lauren Skye describes using menus in her fourth-grade classroom:

While the students are working on their menus I have the opportunity to work in small reading groups with five or six students at a time. Having such a small group has allowed me to focus on my troubled readers and bring them up to speed.

Menus include activities for students to carry out during the week. The activities may include both "must do's" and options to choose from. As with center work, the activities must be ones that students can carry out without teacher support, in their zones of actual development. Each activity should serve a clear academic purpose; for example, to practice or extend a newly acquired skill but not to overdrill it. The activities should help the teacher identify students' trouble spots. Teachers should make sure students routinely get feedback on their menu activities. Teachers must also ensure that menus are not used as a new way of packaging such busywork as packets of worksheets.

Individual conferences give teachers a key opportunity to intervene and provide feedback. These conferences can take many forms. When Wendy Smithers finds that one of her students is "slipping," she holds a quick "mini-conference," looking at portfolio samples and comparing them to the student's recent work, then ending with goal setting. An individual conference might be a social conference, where teacher and student discuss and come to a shared understanding of how the student's participation can be improved with a system of support. It might be a reading conference, where the teacher discusses a student's book preferences, asks for a retelling of what the student has been reading, or focuses on a strategy for figuring out an unknown word. It might be a written conversation with a beginning writer, where the teacher writes a question to a student, the student answers, and a written dialogue ensues. It might be an individual conference during writer's workshop, focusing on how to revise. It might be supported reading, where the teacher listens to a student read, highlights what the student is doing well, and does some on-the-spot work with words. There are as many kinds of individual conferences as there are learners and subjects to be learned.

By making open-ended comments and observations and asking open-ended questions, teachers can show their interest and invite conversation. An open-ended question is one that does not have a yes-or-no answer: "Tell me about your work." "How did you make that?" The best approach is for the teacher to talk genuinely with students about their work, showing authentic curiosity and interest, without a preconceived agenda. This kind of talk comes with practice as teachers relax and discover how much they can learn about children's thinking by just asking.

Teachers must create and maximize opportunities to reach students at their particular levels of need. While students work independently, a teacher can circulate around the classroom and assess students, using clipboards or notebooks to make anecdotal records or observations of students at work.

Sometimes students learn best from individual conferences with the teacher. At other times they need to work in small groups with teacher guidance, or with their peers. Sometimes students' time in the learning zone can best be realized in a whole-group setting, led by the teacher. A balanced daily routine lets students work in these three ways, maximizing their time in the learning zone while letting them work at their own independent levels.

Give Students Clear Instruction and Guidance

The practice of offering behavior to imitate dates back to the beginnings of human society. Modeling begins with interactions with infants and continues into adulthood. The importance of modeling strategies and methods in depth over time cannot be overemphasized. Brian Cambourne (1988), like Vygotsky, found that modeling and demonstration play a critical role in literacy learning: "Learners need to receive many demonstrations of how texts are constructed and used." In modeled reading or writing, the teacher uses her own work as an example for students. During read-alouds, the teacher can pause and share her own reflections or questions about the text. Students see their teacher transact with the text, acting as a reflective reader by making meaning as she reads. Rather than take for granted that students can skim through nonfiction and find the information they need for a particular inquiry, the teacher can "show, not tell" by writing a letter, making a work plan, or taking notes on an instructional video. The teacher's activities give students a window into her mind and thought processes.

In direct instruction, the teacher has a specific lesson to teach—something new or something students are grappling with. In a learner-centered classroom, direct instruction takes the form of short, focused lessons, with the teacher making a presentation. Writer's workshop uses a brief lesson before individual or small-group work. This lesson is focused instruction carried out with the whole group. Such lessons might touch on procedures, writing strategies, the qualities of good writing, or skills. Particularly at the beginning of the year, learner-centered classes spend time on procedural lessons and practice. Their reading lessons might relate to learning about cueing systems, reading strategies, or literary elements. It is critical to student learning that teachers make lessons brief and responsive to students' needs.

Nancie Atwell (2000) has her students take notes on lessons and develop their own writing handbooks. Interacting with a lesson by making a handbook or having another immediate opportunity for practical application can add depth and meaning to the student's learning experience.

Know What, How, and Why You Will Teach

Donald Graves talks about teaching his own craft:

> Teaching writing well is no different than teaching any other subject. The teacher has to know the subject, the process, the children, and the means for the children to become independent learners. (1983, 11)

Knowing the subject area means taking guidance from professionals and experts in the disciplines and subjects we teach. We need to look to the reading researchers we respect, the historians who can teach us about historical thinking, the scientists who show us how they approach a problem. When we can let the rigor of the subject and discipline guide our class studies, we can avoid the pitfalls of "superficiality and factoids" (Palmer 1998). We can communicate expectations for high-quality work to our students: "This is what scientists do." "This is what it means to be professional about writing." "This is what good readers do."

Knowing what you will teach also means knowing the subject matter. Good teaching depends on it. As Caine and Caine point out:

> This does not mean that the teacher must know all the answers. It means the teacher has a "natural," lively grasp of the facts and also engages in discovery. In other words, the teacher models the fact that real experts also continue to learn. (1991, 136)

The teacher's attitude of being a colearner on a voyage of discovery permeates the learning-centered classroom. Some of the themes or subjects we teach best mirror our own interests as learners. With so many subjects to teach, many teachers work with partners or in teams so they can enjoy their own "personal best" subjects while others teach their best areas.

Construct a Classroom with Optimal Learning Conditions

Establishing a balanced daily routine in a learning community is conducive to both teaching and learning. Building the day around blocks of time such as reader's workshop, writer's workshop, project time, or inquiry workshop can make the community's days consistent. Ann Park, like many learner-centered teachers, uses a workshop to teach literacy. A workshop model (Atwell 1987; Calkins 1986) affords optimal working conditions for students and teacher, allowing for both a balanced daily routine and flexible groups. The teacher can continually assess students' work and use a variety of teaching strategies within a climate of respect, cooperation, and hard work. Having a workshop routine allows the teacher to pay attention to instruction and intervention and to keep expectations clear and high. Students know what to expect and are ready to learn.

A workshop in a learner-centered classroom functions like other aspects of a learner-centered classroom:

- Teachers model and demonstrate strategies in depth and over time.
- Teachers provide direct instruction through mini-lessons.
- Students routinely have time for teacher and peer feedback and response, including coaching and guidance at the instructional level.

- Teachers provide extended time for students to engage in authentic practice.
- Students have clear expectations for routines and outcomes.
- Students regularly have time to reflect back, assess new knowledge, and rethink prior assumptions.
- Over time, teachers release responsibility for their own learning and the functioning of the class to students.
- Students increasingly take on responsibility for their own learning by making choices and making their voices heard.

Shifting from teacher-led activities to teacher-guided and student self-guided activities is key to developing students' independence. By using grouping strategies and leadership roles thoughtfully, teachers can gradually release responsibility for learning to the students while giving them the scaffolding they need to become independent.

To construct a classroom that affords optimal learning conditions for students, teachers need time to interact and collaborate, and time to process and reflect. Most of us find the time to reflect as we drive to and from school—or lie awake at night. It is rare for teachers to be given time during the school day to reflect and process with their peers. Some create such time themselves by meeting in support groups at someone's home or by teaming with another teacher. Fifth-grade teacher Marina Chiappellone treasured her cup of tea at the end of each day with her friend and colleague Sandra DeGroot.

Teachers need working conditions that let them provide students with learning communities—the working conditions that other professionals are afforded. Media coverage, politician's speeches, and inadequate salary scales to the contrary, we are professionals. We are in the teaching profession, which means we are expected to exercise our best professional judgment. Lee Shulman, president of the Carnegie Foundation for the Advancement of Teaching, agrees:

> I have concluded that classroom teaching is perhaps the most complex, most challenging, and most demanding, subtle, nuanced, and frightening activity ever invented. The only time that the much more highly rewarded field of medicine even approaches the complexity of an average day of classroom teaching is in an emergency room during a natural disaster. (1987)

Visualize a politician standing in the ER telling the physician how and where to stitch and how many minutes to spend stitching. A different attitude applies to our profession.

The term "best practices" is derived from the medical profession. "In my best judgment,..." "What the best practitioners in this field recommend is..." Yet imagine calling a doctor about a stomachache, then finding twenty to thirty-five others who also have stomachaches when you arrive for your appointment. The doctor appears, opens a medical text, begins with a short reading on abdominal pain, holds a short question-and-answer period, then sends all clients out the door with the same prescription. This is clearly not "best practice." Teachers are told they can follow a similar sequence and meet the needs of their students, but we know that the lives and futures of our "clients"—our students—are no less at stake than the lives and futures of a doctor's patient.

Underfunded, understaffed, and often demoralizing school environments can make it hard for teachers to hold on to high professional standards. We are increasingly driven to teach to standardized tests on the local, state, and national levels and scripted programs are presented to us as being "silver bullets." Teaching a standardized text does not necessarily amount to teaching to meaningful standards—it often translates into very little permanent learning. "In my district, I'm expected to cover five literary elements a week. . ." a new teacher laments. True teaching means covering a skill or topic in depth over time.

The teachers whose learner-centered classrooms are described in this book and many other teachers have a professional commitment to provide students with the support and skills they need to become independent as readers, writers, and thinkers—to create communities that are centered on learning. These teachers' personal authority and rapport with each child move students to exert their personal best. Academic engagement within a supportive, organized physical environment gives students the chance to achieve long-lasting learning, and time spent building respect among students gives them a sense of belonging. Teachers are the decisive factor in our classrooms. We need and deserve support from our school sites, districts, and state education departments—support to be the professionals we can be and to create the learner-centered classroom communities that help students truly learn.

References

Atwell, N. 1987. *In the Middle: Writing, Reading, and Learning with Adolescents.* Portsmouth, NH: Heinemann.

—————. 2000. Teaching Writing in a Workshop. Paper presented at a Heinemann writing workshop, 25 February, Oakland, CA.

Ayers, B. 1998. "An Unconditional Embrace." *Teaching Tolerance* 7 (1): 11–13.

Baylor, B. 1986. *The Way to Start a Day.* New York: Aladdin Books.

Bear, D. R., M. Invernizzi, S. Templeton, and F. Johnston. 2000. *Words Their Way: Word Study for Phonics, Vocabulary, and Spelling Instruction.* 2d ed. Upper Saddle River, NJ: Prentice-Hall, Inc.

Berk, L. E., and A. Winsler. 1995. *Scaffolding Children's Learning: Vygotsky and Early Childhood Education.* Washington, DC: National Association for the Education of Young Children.

Bloome, D. 1987. "Reading as a Social Process in a Middle School Classroom." In D. Bloome (Ed.). *Literacy and Schooling.* Norwood, NJ: Ablex.

Bredekamp, S., and C. Copple, eds. 1997. *Developmentally Appropriate Practice in Early Childhood Programs.* rev. ed. Washington, DC: National Association for the Education of Young Children.

Bruner, J. S. 1966. *Toward a Theory of Instruction.* Cambridge, MA: Harvard University Press.

Caine, R. N., and G. Caine. 1991. *Making Connections: Teaching and the Human Brain.* Alexandria, VA: Association for Supervision and Curriculum Development.

Calkins, L. M. 1986. *The Art of Teaching Writing.* Portsmouth, NH: Heinemann.

Cambourne, B. 1988. *The Whole Story: Natural Learning and the Acquisition of Literacy in the Classroom.* Richmond Hill, Canada: Scholastic-TAB.

Carson, R. 1956. *A Sense of Wonder.* New York: Harper and Row.

Chapman, M. 2000. "Support to Independence." In *Primary Program: A Framework for Teaching*. British Columbia, Canada: Ministry of Education: 84.

Charney, R. S. 1992. *Teaching Children to Care: Management in the Responsive Classroom*. Greenfield, MA: Northeast Foundation for Children.

Cohen, E. G. 1994. *Designing Groupwork: Strategies for the Heterogeneous Classroom*. New York: Teachers College Press.

Cuffaro, H. K. 1994. *Experimenting with the World: John Dewey and the Early Childhood Classroom*. New York: Teachers College Press.

Curwin, R. L., and A. N. Mendler. 1988. *Discipline with Dignity*. Alexandria, VA: Association for Supervision and Curriculum Development.

Delpit, L. 1995. *Other People's Children*. New York: The New Press.

Developmental Studies Center. 1996. *Ways We Want Our Class to Be: Class Meetings That Build Commitment to Kindness and Learning*. Oakland, CA: Developmental Studies Center.

Dewey, J. 1902. *The Child and the Curriculum*. Chicago: University of Chicago Press.

Diamond, M., and J. Hopson. 1998. *Magic Trees of the Mind*. New York: Penguin Group.

Dooley, N. 1991. *Everybody Cooks Rice*. New York: Scholastic Press.

Edelsky, C. 1986. *Writing in a Bilingual Program: Habia Una Vez*. Westport, CT: Greenwood Publishing Group, Inc.

Fosnot, C. T. 1991. *Inquiring Teachers, Inquiring Learners*. New York: Teachers College Press.

Gibbs, J. 1995. *T⁓ ₂s: A New Way of Learning and Being Together*. Sausalito, CA: CenterSource Systems.

Ginott, H. 1971. *Teacher and Child*. New York: Macmillan.

Goodman, Y. M. 1991. "Kidwatching." In *The Whole Language Catalog*. Ed. T. Goodman, L. B. Bird, and Y. M. Goodman. Santa Rosa, CA: American School Publishers.

Goodman, Y. M., and K. S. Goodman. 1990. "Vygotsky in a Whole Language Approach." In *Vygotsky and Education*. Ed. L. C. Moll. New York: Cambridge University Press.

Graves, D. 1983. *Writing: Teachers and Children at Work*. Portsmouth, NH: Heinemann.

————. 1994. *A Fresh Look at Writing*. Portsmouth, NH: Heinemann.

Hogan, K., and M. Pressley. 1997. "Scaffolding Scientific Competencies Within Classroom Communities of Inquiry." In *Scaffolding Student Learning: Instructional Approaches and Issues*. Ed. K. Hogan and M. Pressley. Cambridge, MA: Brookline Books.

Hohmann, M., B. Banet, and D. Weikart. 1978. *Young Children in Action*. Ypsilanti, MI: High/Scope Press.

Hollins, E. R. 1996. *Culture in School Learning: Revealing the Deep Meaning*. Mahwah, NJ: Lawrence Earlbaum Associates.

Howard, J. 1991. *Getting Smart: The Social Construction of Intelligence*. Boston: The Efficacy Institute.

King-Smith, D. 1997. *Babe the Gallant Pig*. Westminster, MD: Knopf.

Kovalik, S., and K. Olsen. 1994. *ITI: The Model, Integrated Thematic Instruction*. Kent, WA: Books for Educators.

Levine, M. D. 1993. *All Kinds of Minds*. Cambridge, MA: Educators Publishing Service.

Lewis, C. C. 1995. *Educating Hearts and Minds: Reflections on Japanese Preschool and Elementary Education*. New York: Cambridge University Press.

Lewis, C. C., E. Schaps, and M. Watson. 1996. "The Caring Classroom's Academic Edge." *Educational Leadership* 54 (1): 16–21.

Malaguzzi, L. 1993. "History, Ideas, and Basic Philosophy: An Interview with Lella Gandini." In *The Hundred Languages of Children*. Ed. C. Edwards, L. Gandini, and G. Forman. Norwood, NJ: Ablex.

Paley, V. 2000. *White Teacher*. Rev. ed. Cambridge, MA: Harvard University.

Palmer, P. 1998. *The Courage to Teach*. San Francisco: Jossey-Bass.

Peterson, R. 1992. *Life in a Crowded Place: Making a Learning Community*. Portsmouth, NH: Heinemann.

Piaget, J. 1965. *The Moral Judgment of the Child*. Trans. M. Gabain. New York: The Free Press. (Original work published 1932.)

————. 1969. *Science of Education and the Psychology of the Child*. New York: Viking Compass.

Piaget, J., and B. Inhelder. 1971. *The Psychology of the Child*. New York: Basic Books.

Project SEED. 1997. "Frequently Used Signals in Project Seed Classes." Berkeley, CA: Project SEED.

Schneps, M. 1989. *A Private Universe: Misconceptions That Block Learning*. Cambridge, MA: President and Fellows of Harvard College. Film.

Shulman, L. S. 1987. "The Wisdom of Practice: Managing Complexity in Medicine and Teaching." In *Talks to Teachers: A Festschrift for N. L. Cage*. Ed. D. C. Berliner and B. V. Rosenshine. New York: Random House.

Skinner, D., D. Bryant, J. Coffman, and F. Campbell. 1998. "Creating Risk and Promise: Children's and Teachers' Co-constructions in the Cultural World of Kindergarten." *The Elementary School Journal* 98 (4): 297–310.

Smith, F. 1988. *Joining the Literacy Club: Further Essays into Education*. Portsmouth, NH: Heinemann.

Tharp, R. G., and R. Gallimore. 1988. *Rousing Minds to Life*. New York: Cambridge University Press.

Valentine, G. 1998. "Lessons from Home." *Teaching Tolerance* 7 (2): 15–19.

Vygotsky, L. 1978. *Mind in Society: The Development of Higher Mental Processes*. Ed. and trans. M. Cole, V. John-Steiner, S. Scribner, and E. Souberman. Cambridge, MA: Harvard University Press.

————. 1986. *Thought and Language*. Trans. A. Kozulin. Cambridge, MA: MIT Press.

Wehlage, G. 1987. "At-Risk Students and the Need for High School Reform." *Education* 107: 18–28.

Weiss, R. 1981. "INREAL Intervention for Language Handicapped and Bilingual Children." *Journal of the Division for Early Childhood* 4: 24–27.

Williams, B. 1998. The Resilient Learner. Paper presented at a professional development workshop, 2 September, Oakland, CA.

Williams, B., and E. Newcombe. 1994. "Building on the Strengths of Urban Learners." *Educational Leadership* 51 (8): 75–78.

Williams, B., and M. Woods. 1997. "Building on Urban Learners' Experiences." *Educational Leadership* 54 (7): 29–32.